P9-DEO-734

Series/Number 07-120

STATISTICAL GRAPHICS FOR VISUALIZING MULTIVARIATE DATA

WILLIAM G. JACOBY
University of South Carolina

SAGE PUBLICATIONS
International Educational and Professional Publisher
Thousand Oaks   London   New Delhi

For information:

SAGE Publications, Inc.
2455 Teller Road
Thousand Oaks, California 91320
E-mail: order@sagepub.com

SAGE Publications Ltd.
6 Bonhill Street
London EC2A 4PU
United Kingdom

SAGE Publications India Pvt. Ltd.
M-32 Market
Greater Kailash I
New Delhi 110 048 India

Printed in the United States of America

Library of Congress Cataloging-in-Publication Data

Main entry under title:

Jacoby, William G.
  Statistical graphics for visualizing multivariate data / by William G. Jacoby.
    p. cm. — (Quantitative applications in the social sciences ; vol. 120)
  Includes bibliographical references.
  ISBN 0-7619-0899-4 (pbk.: acid-free paper)
  1. Multivariate analysis—Graphical methods. I. Title.
  II. Series: Sage university papers series. Quantitative applications in the social sciences ; no. 07-120.
  QA278.J332 1998
  001.4'226—dc21   97-45244

03 10 9 8 7 6 5 4 3 2

When citing a university paper, please use the proper form. Remember to cite the Sage University Paper series title and include the paper number. One of the following formats can be adapted (depending on the style manual used):

(1)JACOBY, W. (1998) *Statistical Graphics for Visualizing Multivariate Data.* Sage University Papers Series on Quantitative Applications in the Social Sciences, 07-120. Thousand Oaks, CA: Sage.
OR
(2)Jacoby, W. (1998). *Statistical graphics for visualizing multivariate data* (Sage University Papers Series on Quantitative Applivations in the Social Sciences, series no. 07-120). Thousand Oaks, CA: Sage.

CONTENTS

ACKNOWLEDGMENTS

This project was supported, in part, by a Research and Productive Scholarship Grant from the University of South Carolina Office of Sponsored Programs and Research. I would like to express my gratitude to Saundra K. Schneider for her untiring support of and many contributions to the monograph. It could not have been completed without her assistance. I would also like to thank Magnugistics Inc., MathSoft Inc., the SAS Institute, the Stata Corporation, and StatSoft Inc. for providing me with copies of their software. Finally, special thanks go to William S. Cleveland and Forrest W. Young. Their excellent work has inspired me and been very influential for my own thinking on statistical graphics and data visualization. Furthermore, they both have been invaluable sources of assistance, advice, and encouragement throughout this project.

SERIES EDITOR'S INTRODUCTION

Data need to be visualized to be understood. That proposition was artfully launched in this series by Professor Jacoby's earlier monograph, *Statistical Graphics for Univariate and Bivariate Data* (No. 117). To help us explore univariate questions, he elucidated histograms, unidimensional scatter-plots, and quartile, box, and dot plots. For bivariate questions, he developed scatterplot enhancements, slicing, and nonparametric smoothing. With his current monograph, he takes the next step, to graphical displays of multi-variate data. This step is logical, although potentially difficult. Relation-ships exist in three or more dimensions, but how to picture them on a sheet of paper, a two-dimensional space? In tackling this problem, Professor Jacoby reveals his deep mastery of graphic techniques.

Reassuringly, he begins with a method we all know—identifying points in a bivariate scatter by values on a third variable. Suppose, for example, policy analyst Dr. Betty Brown is examining the relationship between welfare expenditures, X, and poverty level, Y, in the American states. In the scatterplot for Y on X, with a sample of the 50 states, she might wish to incorporate the third variable of region (South-Nonsouth). She denotes the Southern states with one symbol, say "+," and Nonsouthern states with another symbol, say ">." Professor Jacoby quickly moves from these simple exercises to multiple-code plotting of symbols, such as a "glyph," a circle with a line coming out of the center. The larger the circle or the longer the line, the greater the variable value.

From standard statistical textbooks, we are familiar with the trivariate scatterplot, used to illustrate the least squares principle when there are two independent variables. That picture, meant to extend the analogy of fitting a line in a bivariate scatterplot, is not always rendered intuitively. Professor Jacoby's exposition makes the graph easy enough. First, he draws the whole three-dimensional cube, then he varies the size of the symbols according to distance from the viewing point. Finally, vertical lines connect these points to the "floor" of the cube. In this way, the student comes to see the three-dimensional plot, rather than merely imagining it.

Other important advances in the use of the scatterplot are offered. One is the "scatterplot matrix," a series of bivariate scatterplots in a matrix. By showing all possible bivariate plots at once, the research worker gets an immediate, comprehensive data picture. This represents an improvement over the traditional correlation matrix, because linearity is not assumed. A difficulty remains, however. All the variables are seen, but only two at a time, so the multivariate structure is still hidden. To get at that structure, the analyst needs "conditioning plots," looking at the relation between X and Y while holding Z constant. There are three kinds: casement displays, coplots, and trellis displays. With each, the idea is to illustrate the relationship between X and Y for different "panels," or "slices," of values on Z. It is analogous to physical control in tabular analysis, where a sample is divided into two or more groups before inspection of the relevant statistics.

Finally, Professor Jacoby illustrates observations and variables together, in the "biplot." Here, correlations between variables are revealed by the angle of their vectors, and the similarity of the observations is revealed by the closeness of their dots. Further, the vectors aim themselves at the biggest scores. This and the other methods of the monograph may seem diverse; nevertheless, they are united in that they all picture multiple dimensions in two-dimensional space. These pictures, clearly done and outside constraints from usual statistical assumptions, can expose hidden data structure. Serious researchers should use such graphs, and when they do, their presentations will be immensely aided by consultation of this elegant volume.

—*Michael S. Lewis-Beck*
Series Editor

STATISTICAL GRAPHICS FOR VISUALIZING MULTIVARIATE DATA

WILLIAM G. JACOBY
University of South Carolina

1. INTRODUCTION

This monograph will examine graphical displays that are useful for visualizing multivariate data. As such, it will pick up the discussion that was begun in the companion volume within this series, *Statistical Graphics for Visualizing Univariate and Bivariate Data* (Jacoby, 1997). The basic objective here is to obtain pictorial representations of quantitative information. Multivariate data pose special challenges for statistical graphics, beyond those encountered with univariate or bivariate data. The central problem is to represent information that can vary along *several* dimensions (typically, one for each variable) in a display medium that is almost always inherently *two*-dimensional in nature—a printed page or a computer display.

The Challenge of Multivariate Data: An Example

To illustrate the kinds of problems that can occur with multivariate data, let us consider a simple example. Table 1.1 contains a partial matrix of hypothetical data. The full dataset from which this information is drawn consists of 390 observations on each of three variables. Assume that we are interested in determining whether the third variable (Y) is related to either or both of the first two variables (X_1 and X_2). Of course, it is impossible to interpret these data in their original form; there is simply too much information to comprehend. It is necessary, therefore, to obtain a summary of the information contained in the dataset. There are two general strategies for doing so. We could calculate numerical summaries, in the form of descriptive statistics, or we could create graphical summaries of the data by constructing pictorial displays. As explained in the companion volume

1

TABLE 1.1
Partial Data Matrix, Simulated Data

| Observation | Variable | | |
	X_1	X_2	Y
1	10	10	–2.0
2	8	8	–1.0
3	1	4	–1.5
4	8	8	2.5
5	9	4	2.5
6	6	4	1.0
7	3	6	1.5
8	7	7	0.0
9	2	2	–3.5
10	6	6	3.5
11	8	7	–0.5
12	9	4	–2.5
13	2	2	–4.5
14	4	4	1.0
15	9	10	–0.5
.	.	.	.
.	.	.	.
.	.	.	.
.	.	.	.
376	7	7	–4.0
377	10	7	–1.5
378	5	5	4.5
379	4	4	2.0
380	8	8	2.0
381	7	7	–3.0
382	2	2	1.5
383	8	1	–3.5
384	6	10	–2.0
385	8	8	–4.5
386	5	8	–1.5
387	7	7	0.0
388	1	1	0.0
389	3	3	0.0
390	1	1	–2.0

(Jacoby, 1997), the latter approach requires fewer assumptions about the data; therefore, it is the path followed here.

A naive but rather obvious first step is to construct the two bivariate scatterplots of Y on X_1 and X_2, respectively. These are shown in the two panels of Figure 1.1, and the results are identical in each case: The plotting

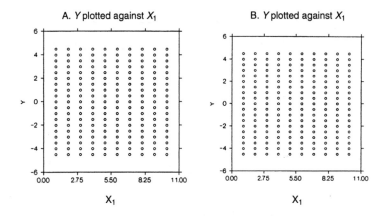

Figure 1.1. Bivariate Scatterplots for Simulated Multivariate Data

symbols are laid out in a rectangular grid, suggesting a "shapeless" cloud of data points. Thus, there appears to be no systematic structure linking either of the X variables to the Y variable. This conclusion appears to be confirmed by the summary statistics for these data: The bivariate correlations between X_1 and Y, and between X_2 and Y, are both equal to zero. Furthermore, the multiple regression of Y on X_1 and X_2 also produces a model with estimated coefficients of zero, and $R^2 = 0.00$. The visual and the numerical evidence both suggest that there is no functional dependence whatsoever between Y and the two X variables in this dataset.

The preceding conclusion, however, is wrong. Figure 1.2 shows an alternative view of exactly the same dataset that reveals that there is a clear structure among these variables. The figure displays a scatterplot of Y against a new variable, X^*. The latter is formed as a linear combination of X_1 and X_2, as follows:

$$X^* = 0.707\, X_1 - 0.707\, X_2$$

In this display, the data points fall perfectly into a "bisected X" pattern. Note that there is a great deal of overplotting in Figure 1.2; in fact, each visible plotting symbol actually corresponds to 10 data points. In any event, this dataset actually conforms to a deterministic, albeit somewhat complicated, multivariate structure. Substantively, this pattern probably would be interpreted as three distinct subsets of observations, each of which is

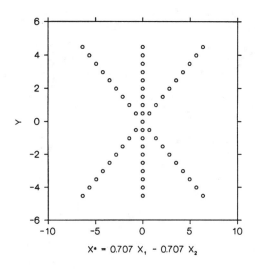

Figure 1.2. Bivariate Scatterplot of Simulated Data, Showing Y Plotted Against a Linear Combination of X_1 and X_2

characterized by a different kind of functional dependence between Y and the two X variables.

The conclusion to be drawn from this simple example is straightforward but important: Graphical displays that are designed for bivariate data can produce misleading results when they are applied to data that contain relatively complex structures and/or vary in several ways, simultaneously. To deal effectively with such situations, it is important to employ graphical methods that explicitly take the multivariate nature of the data into account.

The Concept of a Data Space

The particular challenge for statistical graphics posed by multivariate data stems from the multiple sources of variability within (or more succinctly, the multiple dimensions of) the information under investigation. Indeed, the problem is so pervasive that some analysts have referred to "the curse of dimensionality" (e.g., Bellman, 1961; Fox, 1997; Friedman, 1987) as one of the most serious impediments to effective multivariate analysis. In any event, equating variables to dimensions immediately suggests that a geometric approach might be a useful way to think about multivariate data. Let us consider this idea in greater detail.

According to data theory (e.g., Jacoby, 1991; Young, 1987), a typical rectangular data matrix contains two *ways*. Informally, each "way" corresponds to one of the sides of the tabular data array. One way (usually the rows) represents the observations, while the other way (usually the columns) represents the variables. A geometric depiction of the data—a data space—can be obtained by showing the elements in one way as points or vectors that are plotted within a space that is defined by the elements of the other way in the data matrix. Thus, observation-points are commonly displayed within a coordinate system that is based on the variables.[1] Note that there is a one-to-one correspondence between the marginal elements of the data matrix and the geometric elements of the data space: There is a single point for each observation, and there is a single orthogonal coordinate axis for each variable.

Now, if the data are univariate or bivariate, it is easy to "draw a picture" of the data space, in the form of a scatterplot. Multivariate data, however, consist of n observations with values on each of k different variables (usually designated as X_1, X_2, and so on, to X_k), where k is greater than 2. It would take a scatterplot with k orthogonal axes to locate the observation-points relative to each other, while still maintaining complete fidelity to the original, numeric data. From a mathematical perspective, k-dimensional geometry is no problem whatsoever (e.g., Jacoby, 1991; Weisberg, 1974). From the standpoint of human perception and understanding, however, the potentially extreme multidimensionality of multivariate data causes serious difficulties.[2] We live in a three-dimensional physical world (four-dimensional, if time is taken into account) and most display media are two-dimensional. Therefore, it is impossible to draw a complete picture of the entire k-dimensional data space.

There are two general approaches for dealing with this problem. First, multivariate statistical methods can be used to "distill" the information in the data matrix and reduce it to a more comprehensible form. Procedures like principal components, factor analysis, multidimensional scaling, and correspondence analysis often are employed specifically as dimensionality reduction tools (e.g., Gower & Digby, 1981; Greenacre, 1984; Weller & Romney, 1990). It is important to emphasize that virtually all multivariate statistical techniques, such as regression and ANOVA, can be interpreted in a similar manner (e.g., Gnanadesikan, 1997; Wickens, 1995). The weakness with this approach, as pointed out in the companion volume (Jacoby, 1997), is that all statistical models are built on a foundation of assumptions concerning the nature of any structure that exists within the data. Yet it is precisely this structure that is in question—almost certainly, it is unknown at the outset of the analysis. If the researcher's assumptions are wrong, then any conclusions and inferences about the data are compromised.

The second approach is to devise methods for "looking into" the data space itself. Even though physical limitations preclude a single all-encompassing view of multivariate data, it may be possible to find a viewing perspective on some particularly interesting subset of the data space, one that provides useful insights about the structure underlying the empirical observations. Alternatively, several displays of different "regions" within the data space might be grouped and viewed together in ways that provide more information than each of the displays taken separately. Both of these strategies are intended to provide direct observation of the data, without the "distillation" and attendant loss of detail that invariably accompanies the application of a statistical model.

Notice how the hypothetical example from the previous section exemplifies the two approaches, along with their strengths and weaknesses. The traditional approach—fitting a numeric statistical model—failed miserably. The problem is that tools like bivariate correlation coefficients and a multiple regression equation presuppose the existence of a single, underlying linear structure; this was just not the case in the hypothetical dataset.

Graphical approaches are intended to provide more flexibility and overcome precisely this kind of stringent assumption. In the example given above, however, they also seemed to fail at first. Recall that the bivariate scatterplots shown in Figure 1.1 were very misleading displays of the data. What happened? Stated simply, those particular graphical displays did not take the multivariate nature of the data into account. Any pictorial representation of a k-dimensional data space requires projecting the data points onto a two-dimensional surface, but the "shape" of the projected points is determined by the specific surface that is used, and this has a profound effect on any subsequent interpretation of the data.

In this case, $k = 3$; therefore, the geometric space for the hypothetical data is three-dimensional, with coordinate axes formed by variables X_1, X_2, and Y. Now, the data points can vary across all three of the dimensions, simultaneously. A bivariate scatterplot uses a viewing surface that is parallel to a plane formed by two of the variable axes; therefore, it effectively ignores any variation in the observations' relative positions along the third variable axis. Stated differently, the bivariate scatterplot uses a viewing direction that is orthogonal to the subspace defined by the

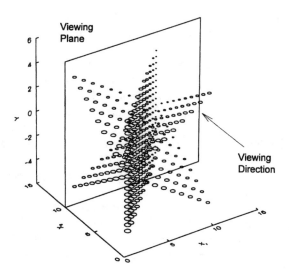

Figure 1.3. Three-Dimensional Scatterplot of Simulated Data, Showing the Viewing Direction and Viewing Surface Used in Figure 1.1A

two variables in the plot; any differences among the data points that occur parallel to this viewing direction will be invisible in the two-dimensional graphical display.

This problem is illustrated in Figure 1.3, which shows a perspective view of the full, three-dimensional data space. It also illustrates the viewing direction and the viewing surface for the bivariate scatterplot from Figure 1.1A. Unfortunately, the most interesting features of the data are invisible on this surface. The two-dimensional scatterplot makes no provision for the changing distances of the data points from the observation position; therefore, the sloping planes on which the data points are arrayed are completely invisible in the resultant graphical display (i.e., Figure 1.1).

The solution, of course, is to find another viewing perspective that does reveal useful information about the structure within the data. Thus, Figure 1.4 shows the viewing direction on the three-dimensional data space that was used to discover the "bisected X" shape within the data; that is, the perspective that was used to produce Figure 1.2. Now, the two-dimensional surface that forms the graph does not correspond to either of the individual X variables within the dataset. Instead, the viewing angle (and hence, the viewing surface) falls midway between the X_1Y plane and the X_2Y plane.

From this position, the observer is looking directly at the "edges" of the flat surfaces that contain the data points. The three intersecting planes within the data, therefore, are clearly visible.

In this simple example, the "correct" viewing angle is known because the data are, themselves, artificially constructed. Of course, this will not be the case in most real data analysis contexts. From a practical standpoint, it makes a great deal of sense to construct graphical displays using the individual variables, just as is done with a bivariate scatterplot; after all, the variables represent a known and substantively interpretable partitioning of the information contained within the full data matrix.

It is important, however, to recognize that the viewing perspective on a multivariate data space is really an arbitrary decision. The problem confronting the researcher is to find the most *useful* perspective(s) from among the infinite number of possible views that could be employed to look at the data under investigation, regardless of whether they correspond to individual variables or not. Graphical displays for multivariate data provide strategies for achieving precisely this objective.

Conclusions

The data space is a useful concept for organizing the presentation of multivariate graphical displays. On one hand, such a geometric model provides a common metaphor that links a number of superficially different methods. The remainder of this monograph discusses a variety of techniques for "looking into" a multidimensional space, in order to observe multivariate data. On the other hand, the notion of a multidimensional space also provides a constant reminder of the challenges that confront the researcher seeking to employ multivariate graphical displays. It is often very difficult to obtain a useful "picture" of phenomena that vary in ways exceeding the capacity of physical representation; therefore, it usually requires some creativity (as well as several attempts) to come up with an adequate representation of phenomena that do not really "fit" within the everyday, three-dimensional world of human observation and perception.

It is important to emphasize the continuity between the topics that will be discussed in this monograph and the material that was presented in *Statistical Graphics for Visualizing Univariate and Bivariate Data* (Jacoby, 1997). Most of the techniques covered below are straightforward generalizations of graphical displays that were introduced in the companion volume, particularly the two-dimensional scatterplot. The objectives of graphical data analysis also remain unchanged. Such methods are useful for exploring the contents of a dataset, finding structure in data, checking underlying assumptions in statistical models, and communicating results from an analysis. The overall graphical approach is identical regardless of whether one is examining univariate, bivariate, or multivariate data (Cleveland, 1993b). Stated briefly, it generally involves an iterative process of *plotting* (to display the basic information itself) and *fitting* (to try out relatively parsimonious structures that summarize the basic information within the complete set of data points).

Finally, the graphical displays that are used for these purposes should seek to optimize the three central components of graphical perception (Cleveland, 1993a): initial visual *detection* to discern individual data points, effective visual *assembly* of individual plotted objects into more general structures, and accurate visual *estimation* of quantitative differences among data objects. Attention to these concerns will help ensure that graphical representations of data really do convey effectively all the interesting information contained within a set of observations and variables.

The remainder of this monograph will be organized as follows. The next two chapters will discuss several methods for coding information directly into the plotting symbols used to represent the observations. Chapter 4 will consider pictorial representations of three-dimensional space. After that, Chapter 5 will discuss the scatterplot matrix as a way of "flattening out" the multiple dimensions of a multivariate data space. Next, Chapter 6 examines conditioning plots, which are strategies for "looking into subregions" of the multidimensional data space. Chapter 7 presents the biplot as a technique for showing observations and variables together in a single display. The last chapter discusses some general ideas about data visualization. It also identifies some methods and strategies that are not covered in this monograph, due to space limitations. Finally, the Appendix discusses statistical software options for graphical approaches to data analysis.[3]

In closing this introduction, it probably is useful to say a few words about the data that will be employed in the chapters below. Virtually all the examples involve social and political characteristics of the American states. In part, this is due to the research interests of the author; however, state-level data of this kind are very useful because they are readily recognizable and understandable to people from many different academic disciplines and substantive backgrounds. Readers can rest assured that the techniques and display methods discussed below are immediately generalizable to virtually any other kind of data that one might encounter in actual research situations.

2. MULTIPLE-CODE PLOTTING
SYMBOLS IN SCATTERPLOTS

Traditionally, graphical displays have conveyed quantitative information by varying the *locations* of objects—for example, the plotting symbols in a scatterplot, the bars in a histogram, and so on. The human "consumers" of statistical graphics, however, usually interpret locations in physical terms, such as depth, height, and lateral position. The problem is that the perceptual world is three-dimensional, even though the data space under consideration may require more dimensions to fully represent all of the variables. It is therefore impossible to convey information about more than three variables when the latter are encoded into spatial positions, alone.

One strategy for dealing with this potentially serious limitation is to represent the data objects with symbols or icons that contain multiple components. Information is then encoded directly into the features of the icons themselves. Patterns and structure in the data are assessed by examining the physical aspects of the plotting symbols, rather than (or, perhaps, in addition to) their relative positions within the graphical display. The icons can be fairly complex; in other words, each one can contain a sizable number of distinct, variable features. As long as the icons are placed in close proximity to each other within the pictorial display, the human visual perception system is capable of distinguishing surprisingly small details from one symbol to the next (Tufte, 1983). Multiple-code plotting symbols thus can be used to obtain graphical representations of multivariate data.

Multiple-code plotting symbols for communicating quantitative information are definitely not new (Tufte, 1990). They have been a mainstay of presentational graphics for many decades (Schmid, 1983), and they are frequently criticized as an easy strategy for "lying with statistics" (e.g., Huff, 1954; Schmid & Schmid, 1979; Wainer, 1997). The use of icons in serious data analysis contexts is a much more recent innovation, undoubtedly partly because of their frequent misuse in journalistic outlets, along with the more general dearth of graphical displays in technical publications (Cleveland, 1984). There is another, more practical reason: Multiple-code plotting symbols require the hardware and software tools provided by high-resolution computer graphics systems. It is effectively impossible to use pencil and paper to achieve the requisite resolution and detail or to render accurately the fine differences from one icon to the next. Multiple-code plotting symbols, however, are now widely available in most statistical software packages, so this impediment is largely absent.

Even though the objective is to graph multivariate data, it often is useful to begin with the familiar bivariate scatterplot. The latter still provides a very powerful means of conveying information about two quantitative variables, and additional information can be encoded into the plotting symbols (e.g., Tukey & Tukey, 1981). The first step is to divide the full set of k variables into two subsets. Two of the variables (say, X and Y) are designated as "foreground variables," and they are used to construct the scale axes of a two-dimensional scatterplot. The remaining $k - 1$ "background" variables (say, V_3, V_4, . . . V_k) are encoded in the components of the plotting symbol. Thus, an observation's values on the foreground variables (x_i, y_i) set its location within the graphical display, and the background variable values $(v_{3i}, v_{4i}, . . . v_{ki})$ determine the nature or shape of its visual representation.

Incorporating a Categorical Variable

Constructing a graph is particularly straightforward when the data consist of two quantitative variables, with observations subdivided by categorical distinctions. Obviously, the quantitative information is used to construct the axes of the scatterplot (i.e., the foreground variables), and different plotting symbols are used for the various categories. The objective is to select the plotting symbols so that the categories can be distinguished visually, without a great deal of effort. This is not necessarily an easy thing to do, because there are other concerns that must be taken into account when constructing the graph, such as overplotting, the degree of resolution, and the physical size of the graphical display medium.

Empirical research on visual detection of texture suggests that the following set of symbols is particularly effective for plotting categorized data:

o   +   <   s   w

The preceding symbols are easily distinguishable, even when there is a great deal of overlap in the positions of the data points from the various categories (Cleveland, 1993a, 1994). The symbols are listed according to their resistance against overplotting problems; therefore, they should be used in the given order, as needed. That is, if there are only two categories, use the open circle and the plus sign. If there are three categories, those two symbols should be followed by the "less than" symbol, and so on.

12

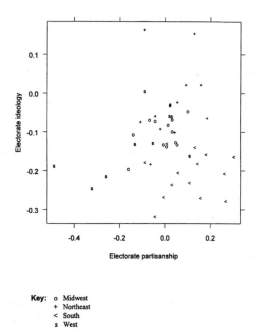

Figure 2.1. Scatterplot of 1992 State Electorate Ideology and State Electorate Partisanship, With Region Shown in Plotting Symbols

SOURCE: Data provided by Gerald C. Wright. More complete explanations of the variables can be found in Erikson, Wright, and McIver (1993).
NOTE: ° = Midwest, + = Northeast, < = South, and s = West. State partisanship is coded so that larger values correspond to more Democratic state electorates. State ideology is coded so that larger values correspond to more liberal state electorates.

Figure 2.1 shows an example of a categorical variable encoded within a bivariate scatterplot. The graph shows 1992 data on the ideology and partisanship of state electorates. The variables are coded so that larger values correspond to states whose citizens describe themselves as more liberal and/or more Democratic and vice versa for states with more conservative and/or Republican electorates.[4] The various plotting symbols are used to represent a four-category regional breakdown, as explained in the graph legend.

Visual inspection of the scatterplot immediately reveals that there are some distinct regional differences in mass-level political orientations. Northeastern states (represented by plus signs) fall in the upper right-hand corner of the graph, indicating that their citizens are relatively liberal and

Democratic. Southern states (shown by the "less than" symbols) fall in the lower-right corner, corresponding to relatively Democratic, but more conservative, electorates. The open circles for the midwestern states cluster near the center, indicating fairly moderate orientations, whereas the "s" symbols for the western states tend to fall in the lower-left segment of the graph (conservative and Republican). In summary, the display shown in Figure 2.1 provides succinct empirical confirmation for some of the "conventional wisdom" about regional variations in American political culture. The example also shows how differences in plotting symbols can be used effectively to represent a third variable in a graphical display, at least when the latter is discrete, with a relatively small number of categories.[5]

Incorporating Several Quantitative Variables

When the researcher is confronted with data that consist entirely of quantitative information, a glyph plot sometimes can provide a useful graphical display of all the variables simultaneously. A "glyph" is defined as a relatively complex plotting symbol that can be varied in different ways to show values on several variables simultaneously (Chambers, Cleveland, Kleiner, & Tukey, 1983; Gnanadesikan, 1997; Tukey & Tukey, 1981). Glyphs are somewhat different from the other icons to be discussed below, because they are explicitly intended to be located within the data region of a two-dimensional scatterplot, in order to represent each observation's values on the set of $k-2$ background variables; again, two of the variables are used in the foreground, to define the scale axes of the scatterplot. Thus, the glyph plot uses several different mechanisms for conveying quantitative information. Each observation's values on the foreground variables (x_i, y_i) set its location within the graphical display, while the background variable values ($v_{3i}, v_{4i}, \ldots v_{ki}$) determine the nature or shape of its plotting symbol.

In principle, there are many different kinds of plotting symbols that could be used. In practice, however, overplotting problems usually lead to relatively simple and compact glyphs. One particularly effective glyph represents each observation as an open circle with a line segment emanating from its center (Wainer & Thissen, 1981). This glyph encodes three separate pieces of information: One variable's value is proportional to the size of the circle; a second variable's value is coded into the length of the line segment, with larger values shown as longer lines and vice versa; and a third variable is represented in the direction of the line segment, so that

14

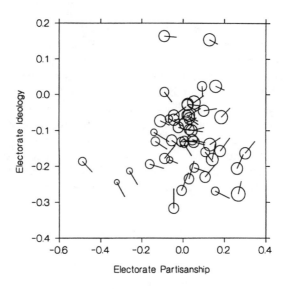

Figure 2.2. Glyph Plot of 1992 State Presidential Voting Results, Plotted Against
Electorate Partisanship and Electorate Ideology

SOURCE: Data provided by Gerald C. Wright. More complete explanations of the variables can be
found in Erikson, Wright, and McIver (1993).
NOTE: Diameter of circle is proportional to Clinton vote percentage. Length of line segment is
proportional to Bush vote percentage. Direction of line segment (clockwise from vertical) is proportional to Perot vote percentage. State partisanship is coded so that larger values correspond to more
Democratic state electorates. State ideology is coded so that larger values correspond to more liberal
state electorates.

the larger the value, the greater the angle from the vertical, 12:00, position,
running clockwise. The display constructed with this kind of glyph is
sometimes called a "vane plot" because the plotting symbols have some
resemblance to weather vanes (Wilkinson, Hill, Micelli, Birkenbeuel, &
Vang, 1992).

Figure 2.2 shows an example of a vane plot, using some data on the
American states. Once again, the foreground variables show 1992 state
electorate partisanship and ideology, just as in Figure 2.1. The three
background variables encoded in the glyphs are state-level voting results
from the 1992 presidential election.[6] The diameter of each circle is proportional to the percentage of the state's popular vote for Bill Clinton in the
1992 presidential election. The length of the line segment emanating from
the center of the circle corresponds to George Bush's 1992 vote percentage.
The direction of the line segment represents the state percentage for Perot.

There are several interesting features in Figure 2.2. Note that the largest circles occur near the right side of the data rectangle. This shows that, as one would expect, Clinton received larger vote percentages in states with relatively Democratic electorates. On the other hand, there does not seem to be much of an ideological component to Clinton's 1992 victory, because the circle sizes do not show much systematic change moving in the vertical direction. Still, this interpretation must remain somewhat tentative, because the empty space in the upper left-hand corner of the data region shows that there were no states with electorates that were simultaneously Republican and liberal in 1992.

Next, consider the voting patterns for George Bush. The line segments in the glyphs tend to get longer as one scans from right to left within the data rectangle, meaning that more Republican electorates returned higher proportions of their respective state votes to Bush. There also is a clear pattern in which the line lengths are greater near the bottom of the display. This shows that states with more conservative electorates provided greater support to Bush than those that were more liberal in composition. The display therefore reveals that there was both a partisan and an ideological caste to 1992 votes for George Bush.

Finally, Figure 2.2 reveals that there were two somewhat distinct sources of electoral support for Ross Perot in 1992. On one hand, he received his strongest support from extremely Republican states: This is shown by the directions of the line segments for the glyphs that fall to the left of the −0.1 position along the horizontal axis; they uniformly point to the right and downward. Surprisingly, however, Perot also received fairly strong support among the states with the most liberal electorates—those that fall at or above the 0.0 position on the vertical axis. Thus, it seems reasonable to conclude that Ross Perot had a detrimental effect on both Clinton and Bush in the 1992 presidential election.

Conclusions

The methods discussed in this chapter show that multivariate information can be displayed using adaptations of the traditional, bivariate scatterplot. This is certainly the great advantage of graphs that employ multiple-code plotting symbols. There are also some potential weaknesses that should be considered. The first problem is of particular concern for categorical variables. The hierarchy of plotting symbols presented above allows for only five separate categories; it does not address the situation in which a variable divides the data into a larger number of discrete subgroups. Fortunately, this problem does not arise very frequently in practice. Discrete ordinal variables usually can be treated as quantitative information for graphical purposes (perhaps with enhancements, like jittering, to improve visual resolution). Discrete nominal variables with more than a handful of separate categories probably are the exception rather than the rule in empirical data; however, when they do occur, it probably is best to divide them across multiple scatterplot panels, rather than trying to use different symbols to represent all the categories in a single display.

A second problem affects both categorical plotting symbols and glyphs. In either case, severe overplotting will almost certainly occur in the scatterplot, thereby inhibiting the visual resolution of the multivariate information. This overplotting is readily apparent, even with the fairly small number of observations employed in Figure 2.2 ($n = 48$); the problems become much more severe with larger datasets. On the other hand, a counterargument is that overplotting usually is worst in the central of the data rectangle and less severe near the edges, but observations that fall within the latter areas are often the most revealing of the functional dependencies that may exist among the variables. For this reason, some analysts suggest that glyph plots can be used for surprisingly large numbers of observations (Friendly, 1991; Nicholson & Littlefield, 1983).

Third, the kinds of glyphs that are most resistant to overplotting problems are precisely those that require relatively difficult visual processing tasks for interpretation. The vane symbols involve judgments about area, relative lengths of nonaligned (and nonparallel) line segments, and angular directions (or slopes). All of these tasks fall relatively low in Cleveland's hierarchy of visual processing accuracy. A closely related problem is the fact that each glyph must be relatively simple in form, so it can encode only a limited number of variables. Glyph plots therefore are practical only when k, the number of variables, is relatively small.

Fourth, the distinction between foreground and background variables—required for glyph plots—is sometimes an artificial one. This is not much of a problem in Figure 2.2, where state partisanship and ideology seem like reasonable independent variables, compared to voting results as dependent variables. In many other cases, however, the analyst may be interested in common structure among the full set of variables, rather than functional dependencies between one subset of variables and another. In that case, it probably is better to treat all of the variables in a more symmetric manner and avoid imposing artificial divisions of any kind on the data. Several display methods for doing so will be discussed in the next chapter.

3. PROFILE PLOTS

Quantitative multivariate data often are depicted in tabular form, as an n (observations) by k (variables) matrix of numeric values. For a given observation, i, the full set of k variable values is often called the *profile* for that observation (e.g., Sneath & Sokal, 1973). When n is not too large, it often is useful to provide a pictorial representation of the full profile for each observation. This can be accomplished using any of several different kinds of multiple-code icons. These kinds of displays are given the generic name *profile plots* (Bertin, 1983), and they differ from the glyph plots considered previously in at least two ways. First, the symbols used to show the profiles can contain a great deal of information—10 variables can be represented very easily, and even larger values of k are not uncommon. Second, the separate icons are laid out in some regular array, rather than positioned according to the values of two foreground variables. This avoids all overplotting problems, accords "equal status" to all k variables, and enables fairly detailed visual inspection of the data.

Histogram Plots

A *histogram plot* represents each observation as a set of k concatenated vertical bars (Freni-Titulauer & Louv, 1984). Each bar corresponds to one of the k variables in the profile. The height of each bar is proportional to the value of that single variable for that particular observation. The ordering of the variables is identical from one icon to the next, to facilitate visual comparisons across the observations.

In this kind of plot, the icon for each observation is reminiscent of a univariate histogram; however, it is important to emphasize that the icon conveys a completely different kind of information. A traditional histogram shows univariate densities; here, the full set of bars in a histogram icon depicts an observation's complete profile across the multiple variables. The histogram icons require an implicit assumption that the k values making up each observation's overall profile can be compared to each other in meaningful ways. Because this frequently is not the case in the raw data, it often is necessary to standardize the variables, or rescale them to a common range of values, before constructing the plot.

Figure 3.1 shows a histogram plot for some state-level data on governmental expenditures.[7] The icons are arranged alphabetically, by state name, into an eight-row by six-column rectangle. The histogram bars represent 1992 per capita state spending in each of five policy areas. Within each

18

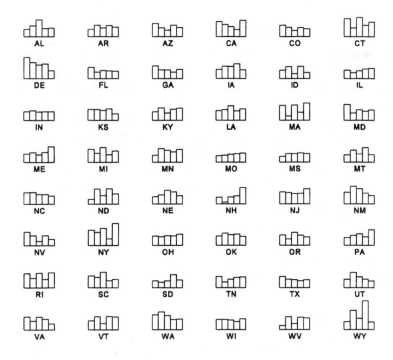

Variable Assignment Key:

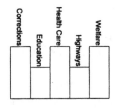

Figure 3.1. Histogram Plot of 1992 State Policy Expenditures

icon, the bars are arrayed alphabetically, according to the first letter of the policy area. From left to right, they are corrections, education, health care, highways, and welfare. Although these variables are all measured in a common unit (dollars per capita), their values are standardized to eliminate variations in bar heights resulting from the different *mean* expenditure values for each of the policy areas. For example, all states spend more on education than on any of the other policy areas. As a result, the second bar from the left (i.e., the one corresponding to education expenditures) would dominate all the icons if the data were left in their original form.

The histogram plot is excellent for visual detection, because it is very easy to interpret the bar heights in terms of relative data values. Thus, Delaware spends a great deal of money in all areas except welfare (as shown by the four high bars on the left of its icon followed by one relatively low bar); Connecticut and Massachusetts concentrate their resources on corrections, health care, and welfare (as indicated by the "pitchfork" patterns of their icons); Indiana and Mississippi both spend almost uniformly small amounts on all five policy areas contained in the graph; and so on. The histogram plot also enables visual estimation of relative data values. As a specific example, consider the icon for Alabama (located in the upper left corner of the display). The tall bar in the center of this histogram can be compared to the other bars in that icon to show that Alabama's standardized spending value for health care is about twice the sizes of the spending values for corrections, highways, and welfare (the first, fourth, and fifth bars from the left, respectively). Furthermore, Alabama's standardized value for education (the second bar from the left) is about two-thirds the size of its health care value. In summary, the histogram plot in Figure 3.1 can be used to discern many specific details about relative state spending levels in the various policy areas.

Unfortunately, the graph in Figure 3.1 is not very useful for assembling the information into overall patterns that may be useful for identifying any underlying structure within the data. Note, however, that this is a deficiency in this particular display, rather than a general limitation of histogram plots. The problem is that the icons and the bars within the icons are both laid out in an arbitrary manner (i.e., alphabetically), which does nothing to highlight potentially interesting features of the variables or the observations. The obvious remedy is to employ some rational scheme to rearrange the features of the display. This step is very important for the interpretation of any icon plot, and it could be applied easily to the histogram display in Figure 3.1. For now, the discussion will simply move on to the next type of graphical display.

Profile or Polygon Plots

Figure 3.2 shows the 1992 state spending data using a slightly different kind of graphical display. There are two important differences from the histogram plot discussed previously. First, the histograms obviously have

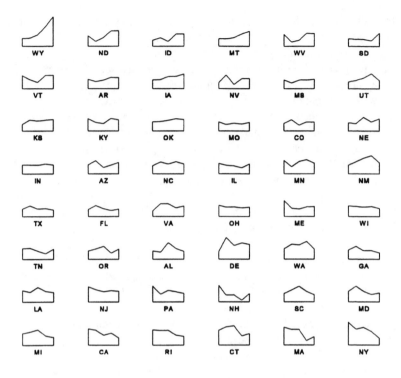

Variable Assignment Key:

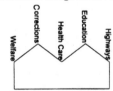

Figure 3.2. Polygon Plot of 1992 State Policy Expenditures

NOTE: State icons are arranged according to their scores on the first principal component from the per capita spending data.

been replaced by polygons. These polygons contain exactly the same information as the histograms; in fact, the former icons can be viewed as adaptations of the latter. Specifically, imagine that the icon for each observation begins as a histogram. Then, a polygon is formed from each histogram by connecting the midpoints of the tops of the histogram bars. These connecting points could be called the vertices of the polygon. Finally, the bars themselves are then omitted from the display. In this manner, variable values for a single observation are still represented by the height of the plotting symbol at each of k points along the horizontal axis of its icon. Interpretation, however, is carried out by scanning the *shapes* of the plotted symbols. This serves to highlight the pattern of values across the respective variables for each observation. In contrast, the bars of the histogram plot implicitly emphasized the separate values of the individual variables. The kind of display shown in Figure 3.2 is often called a *profile plot* (Chambers et al., 1983), but the term *polygon plot* will be used here to distinguish it from the other graphs that display observation profiles.

The second difference is that the graphical components in Figure 3.2 have been arranged in a way that will, we hope, provide greater insight about any structure that may exist within the data. Specifically, the 1992 state spending data were subjected to a principal component analysis (e.g., see the monographs in this series by Dunteman, 1989, or Weller and Romney, 1990). The vertices of each polygon are ordered according to the variables' coefficients on the first principal component. Moving from right to left within each icon, per capita highway spending had the smallest loading, followed by education spending, health care spending, corrections spending, and welfare spending, respectively. Similarly, the icons are also arrayed according to the states' scores on the first principal component. Thus, Wyoming (in the upper left-hand corner) has the smallest score, followed by North Dakota, and so on, down to New York (in the lower right-hand corner). In this manner, the principal components analysis is employed as a seriation method to provide a relatively objective scheme for arranging the components of the graph. Other multivariate techniques, such as factor analysis or multidimensional scaling, could be used for the same purpose.

With this arrangement of the spending areas and the states, there do seem to be some regular patterns that emerge in the display. First, note that many of the states in the upper rows of Figure 3.2 tend to be conservative and Republican in their political orientations (e.g., Wyoming, Idaho, Montana, Mississippi, and so on), whereas many of those in the lower rows are relatively liberal and/or Democratic (e.g., New York, Massachusetts, and Maryland). Second, there also appears to be a geographic basis for the arrangement of the icons. Many of those near the top are large, western states with small populations (such as Wyoming, North Dakota, Nevada, and Utah); states near the bottom of the graph tend to be densely populated (e.g. California, Michigan) and/or relatively small in size (e.g., Rhode Island, Connecticut). Third, there seems to be a fairly systematic change in the shapes of the plotting symbols that occur within the figure. Those near the top of the display show a negative skew. In other words, the icons are taller on their right sides, indicating more spending on highways and education. The symbols near the bottom of the display have a positive skew. Their heights tend to trail off more in a rightward direction, indicating relatively larger amounts of spending on welfare and corrections. States shown in the central rows of Figure 3.2 show a variety of patterns, including many with roughly uniform expenditures across most of the policy areas.

Taken together, the evidence suggests that patterns of state policy spending are affected by both political and geographic considerations. Large states with sparse populations devote resources to highways in order to meet vital transportation needs. Smaller states with more concentrated populations must emphasize human services, such as health care and welfare. Thus, the graphical evidence provided by Figure 3.2 is sufficient to indicate the presence of systematic and substantively reasonable structure within the data.

It is important to exercise some caution when interpreting the results in Figure 3.2. Closer inspection reveals a number of departures from the general pattern. For example, Vermont is a small, relatively liberal state, but its icon falls near the top of the figure. At the same time, South Carolina and New Hampshire are widely regarded as conservative states, but they appear near the bottom of the graph. These and other anomalies in Figure 3.2 suggest that it might be useful to try other arrangements of the data elements to see whether alternative patterns of variability can be found. In fact, this is good advice for any profile plot (Chambers et al., 1983). It is almost always useful to rearrange the components of the graph several times, to find arrays that reveal underlying structure within the data.

Star Plots

When the number of variables in the observation profiles becomes large, the histogram and polygon plots discussed above become somewhat unwieldy. The problem lies in the nature of the icons used in those displays. Each icon is necessarily restricted to a fairly narrow width so that all n icons can be included within a single display. When k is large, however, the horizontal interval allocated to each variable within each icon is forced to be too narrow for accurate visual inspection and interpretation. When this occurs, a *star plot* provides a useful alternative strategy for graphical depiction of observation profiles (Chambers et al., 1983; Friedman, Farrell, Goldwyn, Miller, & Sigel, 1972).

In a star plot, each observation is shown as a collection of k rays emanating from a central point. These rays are equally spaced around the point; the angle between any pair of adjacent rays is therefore $360/k$ degrees. More important, each ray is assigned to a particular variable, and the length of the ray is proportional to the value of the variable for that observation. The terminal points of adjacent arrays usually are connected by line segments. The shape of the resultant icon often resembles a multipointed star, and this feature obviously leads to the name of the display.

As in all profile plots, variables are assigned to the same rays in each of the plotted icons. Similarly, the variables in the display should be standardized, if necessary, to ensure that they are all measured in comparable units. The physical sizes of the rays can be scaled in several different ways, but most software for constructing star plots assigns the smallest value in the data a length of zero. The largest data value then receives the maximum possible length for a ray, and all other rays vary between the two extremes.

Star plots usually can be interpreted very easily. The sizes of the stars show the general magnitudes of the variable values; an observation with a large star has relatively high values on the variables, and vice versa. The shapes of the stars reflect the differences in values across the variables; for example, an observation with a markedly asymmetric star has high values on some variables and low values on others. When the n star icons are juxtaposed to one another within the display, the differences in their shapes and sizes are immediately obvious. Thus, it often is very easy to discern substantively interesting patterns of variability through simple visual inspection.

Figure 3.3 shows a star plot based on public opinion data collected during the 1992 presidential election campaign.[8] The stars represent evaluations of 14 political figures (12 people and the two major parties) made by nine subsets of survey respondents. The subsets reflect various combinations of individual partisan identification (Democratic, independent, and Republican) and ideological self-placement (liberal, moderate, and conservative). Survey respondents rated each of the 14 figures on a scale ranging from 0 to 100, with larger values indicating more positive evaluations. The mean rating scores were calculated within each of the nine subsets and used as the data values to construct the icons in Figure 3.3. Note that these data have not been standardized, because the variables all employ a common scale, with values that can be compared meaningfully across political figures and across subgroups.

24

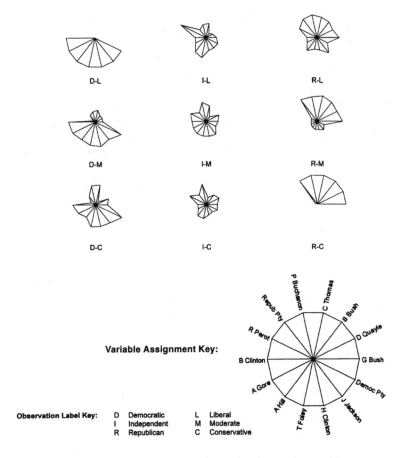

Figure 3.3. Star Plot Showing Mean Evaluations (on 1-100 Rating Scale) of Political Figures Given by Partisan and Ideological Groups Within the 1992 American Electorate

NOTE: D = Democratic, I = Independent, R = Republican; L = Liberal, M = Moderate, and C = Conservative.

In this case, the components of the graph (i.e., the separate stars and the rays within each one) are arranged according to a priori substantive considerations. The stars are laid out in a square grid; the columns of the grid correspond to party identification groups, from Democratic (left column) through independent (middle) to Republican (right column). Similarly, the rows of the grid correspond to ideological groups, from liberal on the top to conservative on the bottom. The key for the figure shows how the rays correspond to the different political figures within each icon. Notice that Republican and conservative stimuli are found in the upper half of each star, whereas Democratic and liberal stimuli occur in the bottom half. The two 1992 major party presidential nominees are placed exactly opposite each other, with Bill Clinton at the "9:00 position" and George Bush at "3:00." Of course, Ross Perot, the independent candidate, does not fit within either of the two partisan categories; therefore, the ray that corresponds to Perot evaluations should be placed in between the respective sets of Republican and Democratic figures. Because there are fewer Republican figures than Democratic in the figure (six, compared to seven Democrats), the ray for Perot is located just above the 9:00 position in Figure 3.3.

A number of interesting features are discernible in Figure 3.3. First, there are very strong partisan influences on these evaluations. The stars for the Democratic subsets (in the top row of the display) are almost perfect mirror images of their respective Republican counterparts (shown in the bottom row). Second, ideology has a separate impact on political evaluations. The polarization of evaluations is most pronounced within the two subsets of individuals whose ideologies are consistent with their partisanship—Democratic liberals and Republican conservatives. Third, the star plot helps clarify the partisan and ideological basis of Ross Perot's public support. Specifically, the most positive evaluations of Perot occur among political independents, as signaled by the particularly long rays at the "10:00 position" on the stars that occur in the center column of the display. Fourth, Democrats and Republicans seem to be happier with the 1992 political figures than are independents. Ignoring asymmetries and looking strictly at ray lengths, it is clear that the longest ones occur in the left and right columns of the display. In summary, the concise display in Figure 3.3 provides an enormous amount of information about political attitudes among various partisan and ideological subgroups within the American electorate.

Conclusions

This chapter has covered a variety of methods for encoding multivariate information into the plotting symbols that are used to construct a graphical display. A number of other multivariate icons and plots can be used, in addition to those discussed here.[9] In every case, the objective is similar: a pictorial representation of the observations contained in a multivariate, quantitative data matrix. It is, perhaps, tempting to dismiss these displays as simplistic novelties; however, doing so would ignore their strengths and their potential power in an exploratory data analysis strategy.

The profile plots discussed in this chapter possess several distinctive strengths. First, these displays show the full configuration of variable values for all the observations in a dataset. In so doing, they present all of the multivariate data, rather than merely summarizing the information. This often is a marked advantage in itself, because data summaries of any kind must rely on assumptions that may or may not be met empirically.

Second, graphical displays that rely on multiple-code plotting symbols (i.e., both icons and the glyphs that were discussed in Chapter 2) place information about a number of variables and observations into close physical proximity. This is important because it facilitates visual identification of patterns within the data. This is particularly useful when the underlying structure involves several distinct variables or has a complex form that cannot be summarized very well with traditional numeric methods.

Third, methods based on multiple-code symbols represent a very flexible approach to a dataset. In other words, it is easy to rearrange the components of these plots to highlight different aspects of the data. With some relatively simple manipulations, the analyst can modify a display to focus on particular observations, a single variable's distribution of relative values across observations, and/or patterns in values across several variables. Thus, icon-based displays can be used to try many different perspectives on the information at hand.

Next, consider the weaknesses that are almost inherent in these kinds of plots. First, data icons definitely are not very useful for conveying information about specific quantities or numeric values. There is simply no way to perform effective table look-up from the kinds of multiple-code symbols discussed in this chapter. On the other hand, this weakness is not terribly serious, because graphs generally are less useful for communicating specific numbers than they are for conveying more general trends and patterns in the data.

A second weakness is that these kinds of displays can contain only a relatively small number of distinct icons or symbols. Only a limited number of separate icons can be displayed usefully in a single histogram, polygon, or star plot. At the same time, visual resolution degrades rapidly when any of these types of plots are used to depict large sets of variables; the plotting symbols or icons are, themselves, quite small relative to the overall size of the graphical display. Therefore, only a finite amount of detail will be visible on any single icon. For practical purposes, these limitations mean that the amount of information to be plotted must be quite small.

This, in turn, leaves the analyst with two possibilities: (a) the original data must contain relatively few variables and observations, as was the case with the state expenditures data used earlier; or (b) the original data must be "pre-processed" to combine variables into multiple-item indices and/or to obtain summary data values, by aggregating within subsets of the original observations (as with the data on party identification, ideology, and the evaluation of political figures). Of course, the latter course of action is somewhat contradictory to the overall objectives of *graphical* analysis, because the data reduction process is dependent on a priori assumptions about the proper ways to aggregate the original observations. It is also subject to the loss of important information from the original variables and/or individual observations.

A third weakness stems from one of the strengths mentioned above. There is no unambiguously "best" way to order the variables within the plotting symbols or to arrange the symbols within the overall display. With even relatively small datasets, it is nearly impossible to try all possible combinations, and it is easy to get overwhelmed by the information after rearranging the data only a few times. As a result, there is always the possibility that the analyst will miss some interesting feature of the data simply because he or she did not "look at them from the optimal vantage point."[10]

Despite these weaknesses, graphical displays that use multiple-code plotting symbols often are capable of displaying a great deal of information in a relatively efficient manner. The contents of an icon plot or a scatterplot with glyph symbols probably should be viewed more as suggestive, rather than conclusive, information. As long as the analyst keeps this caveat in mind, such graphical displays can be very useful for exploring the contents of complicated multivariate datasets.

4. THREE-DIMENSIONAL PLOTS FOR TRIVARIATE DATA

Traditionally, statistics texts have emphasized the differences between univariate and bivariate methods, and also between bivariate and multivariate methods. These distinctions are reasonable, given the different objectives of the various kinds of analyses: Univariate methods seek to describe a single characteristic of the observations, bivariate techniques measure relatively simple relationships between two variables, and multivariate methods seek to reveal more complex structures within the data, usually involving several variables simultaneously. The graphical approach to data analysis certainly does not ignore these differences, but it makes an additional distinction, between multivariate analyses involving three variables and those involving four or more variables. Cleveland (1994) calls these separate situations *trivariate* and *hypervariate* data, respectively. The reason for making the trivariate-hypervariate distinction in graphical data analysis methods is simple: With trivariate data, it is possible to construct a direct physical representation of the complete data space. This cannot be done for datasets containing more than three variables.

Even with trivariate data, it is still necessary to convey the three-dimensional variability on a two-dimensional surface (Gower & Digby, 1981). There are many well-developed methods for doing so, most of which have been developed in fields outside the statistical sciences (Tufte, 1997). Artists have been "tricking" the human visual perception system to achieve precisely this objective for hundreds of years—ever since the principles of perspective drawing were discovered. These same principles can be adapted to display trivariate quantitative data, and they will be discussed in the remainder of this chapter.

Three-Dimensional Scatterplots

Conceptually, the three-dimensional scatterplot is a direct generalization of the two-dimensional scatterplot. As such, it can be used to examine the relationship between a dependent variable (say, Y) and two independent variables (say, X_1 and X_2). Each of these variables is represented by a coordinate axis that is placed perpendicular to the other two. Taken together, the three variable axes form a three-dimensional space that could be called the scale cube for the graph. By convention, Y corresponds to a vertical corner of the cube while X_1 and X_2 are horizontal corners. Each pair of variable axes also defines a plane, which corresponds to a "wall" of the cube. Observations are plotted as points within the interior of the scale cube, with each one located at the intersection of the perpendicular projections from that observation's values along each of the coordinate axes. All of the data points should be located in the interior of the scale cube; none of them should touch any of the planes that form the exterior of the scale cube. Therefore, it is reasonable to think of a data cube, defined as an imaginary region that just contains all the data points.

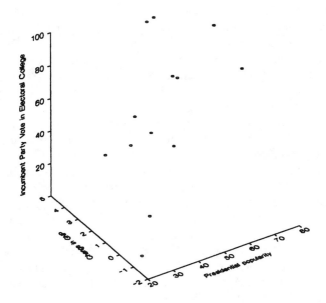

Figure 4.1. Basic Three-Dimensional Scatterplot, Showing Incumbent Party Vote Percentages in the Electoral College as a Function of Presidential Popularity and Change in GNP

Visually, some adjustments must be made to convey the three-dimensional nature of the space containing the data points. This is accomplished by drawing the angles between the coordinate axes at a separation different from 90 degrees. Frequently, the point corresponding to the smallest plotted values on the variables (i.e., the graphical origin) is placed in the fore-ground of the graph. The axes for the variables that form the horizontal plane of the scale cube are then shown with an obtuse angle between them, while the dependent variable's axis is retained in a nearly vertical position. This creates the impression that the viewer's eye is positioned somewhere above the horizontal surface of the data cube, and that the scales for the horizontal variables are arrayed in directions that point away from that viewing position.[11]

Figure 4.1 shows a very basic three-dimensional scatterplot, created on some data pertaining to American presidential elections from 1948 to 1996.[12] The dependent variable (vertical axis) is the electoral college vote percentage received by the candidate from the incumbent political party in each year. There are two independent variables: First, the percentage change in GNP during the previous year is represented by the "horizontal" axis that points toward the upper-left corner of the graph. Second, the incumbent president's public approval rating (measured during the summer before the election) is shown along the other "horizontal" axis—the one that moves from the graphical origin toward the upper-right corner. Note that only three "edges" of the scale cube are shown, to avoid any overplotting of the data points themselves.

If the observer can perceive the illusion of the three-dimensional cube in Figure 4.1, then the structure within these data is fairly obvious: The plotted points tend to fall at higher vertical positions as they are located closer toward the rear of the data cube. This, in turn, suggests that positive changes in GNP and higher levels of presidential popularity both lead to larger electoral college vote percentages for the incumbent party. The problem with this display pertains to the ability to observe the three-dimensional illusion in the first place. There are few depth cues in Figure 4.1 to encourage the visual perception of a cube containing the plotted points. The angular separations of the three axes and the use of ellipses to represent the data points both facilitate the perspective of the display, but there is not much else to reinforce this interpretation. Accordingly, to many observers, the data points simply seem to float in an empty space.

It often is useful to add enhancements to a three-dimensional scatterplot to emphasize the depth illusion (Huber, 1987). Figure 4.2 illustrates several techniques that could be used for this purpose. The display shows the same electoral college voting data as Figure 4.1, but the scale cube and the data points are rendered differently. First, the entire cube is now shown, rather than only three edges, to clarify the perspective view on the data. Second, the sizes of the plotting symbols are now varied systematically, with the ellipses becoming smaller as their distance from the viewing point increases. This, of course, creates the visual illusion of depth. Third, there are now vertical line segments connecting the plotting symbols with the bottom horizontal facet of the scale cube. This depicts the different vertical heights of the data points within the three-dimensional space.

Unfortunately, the three-dimensional scatterplot remains fairly unsatisfactory for analytic purposes, regardless of which visual enhancements are applied to it. The problems with this kind of graphical display can be described in terms of Cleveland's (1993a) visual perception theory. First, visual *detection* will be hampered by the large amount of overplotting that is almost certain to occur with datasets that contain even moderate numbers of observations. This problem will be exacerbated by the kinds of visual enhancements discussed above, because all these devices reduce the data-

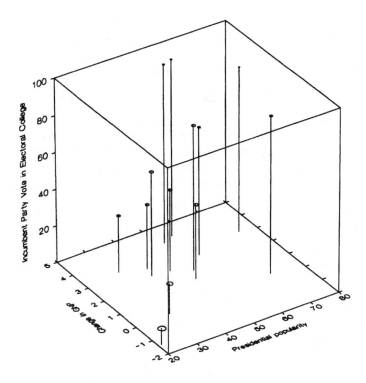

Figure 4.2. Three-Dimensional Scatterplot, Showing Incumbent Party Vote Percentages in the Electoral College as a Function of Presidential Popularity and Change in GNP (display enhanced to emphasize illusion of depth in

ink ratio of the graph, thereby reducing the primacy of the data points themselves (Tufte, 1983).

Second, visual *assembly* is inhibited because it is difficult to discern anything more than very general patterns in the three-dimensional point cloud. In other words, it is almost impossible to make detailed statements about the structure within the data, regardless of the visual enhancements that have been applied to the display. This problem becomes more severe when the clarity of the underlying structure is less pronounced—a situation that occurs whenever there is "noise" variation affecting the plotted points. Unfortunately, the latter problem arises in all empirical data.

Third, it is difficult to achieve accurate visual *estimation* of data values in a three-dimensional scatterplot. Because of the simulated perspective view in the display, the visual perception task required for estimation is comparison of point positions along nonaligned scales. This, in itself, produces less accurate judgments than those involving comparisons along a common scale (like those that would be used in a traditional, two-dimensional scatterplot). The problem is even more severe, because the lack of depth cues makes it difficult to determine exactly *which* nonaligned scales should be used to compare any two plotted points.

For all of the preceding reasons, the three-dimensional scatterplot does not work very well as an analytic graphical display. This conclusion, however, should be qualified in several ways. First, it can be useful as a *presentational* graphic (Schmid, 1983). If the analyst already understands the structure within the data and merely wants to convey their prominent features to some audience, a three-dimensional scatterplot can be very effective for doing so. After all, most people (i.e., those without any training in statistics or data analysis) have a great deal of practice at interpreting perspective displays in pictures—the "leap" to doing the same thing with data is not a terribly difficult task (Kosslyn, 1994).

Second, three-dimensional plots can be useful in situations where data "noise" is not a problem. For example, consider the simulated data shown back in Chapter 1: The deterministic pattern in the plotted points was relatively easy to see in Figure 1.3 precisely because there was no stochastic or otherwise random component to move the points off their respective planar locations. Of course, empirical data always contain some noise, but if noise constitutes a relatively small portion of the overall variability across the observations, then it still may be possible to discern structural patterns in the three-dimensional scatterplot.

Third, a related course of action would be to fit a smooth surface to the noisy data, show a grid representing this surface within the scale cube, and omit the data points from the plot. A smooth surface can be discerned quite clearly in a three-dimensional plot (Cleveland, 1994; Rock, 1984). The surface could be constructed using linear regression (Cook & Weisberg, 1994), multivariate loess (Cleveland, Devlin, & Grosse, 1988), or any other smoothing strategy (Simonoff, 1996), depending on the kinds of assumptions that the researcher is willing to make about the data. The resultant smooth surface plot would display the *structure* in the data without showing the individual observations themselves.

Fourth, the utility of a three-dimensional scatterplot can be increased enormously by adding motion to the display; however, doing so moves the discussion into dynamic, interactive graphics (e.g., Young, Faldowski, & McFarlane, 1993) which are, unfortunately, beyond the scope of this monograph. For present purposes, it is enough to say that "moving" the three-dimensional scale cube, relative to the viewing position, provides very useful cues about depth within the display (e.g., Becker, Cleveland, & Weil, 1988; Huber, 1987; Young, Kent, & Kuhfeld, 1988). This greatly enhances the importance of the three-dimensional scatterplot as an analytic tool.

Bubble Plots

As we have just seen, the visual techniques required to create the perspective view of a three-dimensional scatterplot remove the depth cues that are necessary for making accurate visual judgments about structure within the plotted data. The basic idea of "looking into" the three-dimensional data space nevertheless still seems to be a good one; therefore, it is reasonable to try a graphical display that provides a "partial perspective" view of the data space, that is, one that simulates the depth dimension (which cannot be physically represented on the two-dimensional viewing surface) but still enables accurate visual perception of the quantitative information in the display. This is precisely the idea behind a bubble plot.

The bubble plot begins with a standard, two-dimensional scatterplot, in which values on two quantitative variables are indicated by each observation's position within the scale rectangle of the display. Then, information on a third quantitative variable is encoded into the *size* of the plotting symbol used for each observation. Typically, larger variable values are shown as larger plotting symbols. It is very important to use an open, rather than filled, plotting symbol, because there almost certainly will be some degree of overplotting in the display. Because open circles seem to be the symbols that are most resistant to such problems, they are employed most frequently for this purpose (Chambers et al., 1983). Of course, the resultant visual impression is exactly what leads to the name "bubble plot."

Figure 4.3 shows the electoral college voting data represented as a bubble plot. The scale axes of the graph represent the vote percentage received by the candidate from the incumbent political party (vertical axis) and the percentage change in GNP during the previous year (horizontal axis), respectively. The incumbent president's public approval rating is encoded into the size of the plotting symbol. Specifically, the value of this variable is proportional to the circumference of the plotting symbol. Thus, larger circles correspond to more positive public evaluations of the incumbent president.

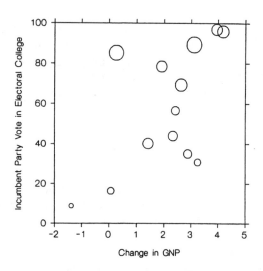

Figure 4.3. Bubble Plot Showing Incumbent Party Electoral College Vote Percentage Versus Change in GNP, With Presidential Popularity Coded Into Diameter of Plotting Symbols

The information in this bubble plot shows that both independent variables have an effect on electoral college outcomes. In general, the plotted circles run diagonally, from lower left to upper right. This indicates that GNP change is positively related to incumbent vote success. The apparent outliers from this predominant pattern are explained by the separate effects of presidential popularity. For example, consider the point that is located closest to the upper left-hand corner of the graph: This is an election in which the incumbent vote was very large, despite only a modest change in the GNP. The large circle for this data point shows that presidential popularity was extremely high that year. Conversely, the point located closest to the lower right-hand corner represents a year in which the incumbent vote percentage was very small, despite a large, positive change in GNP. This occurs because presidential popularity was unusually low in that election, as shown by the small size of the circle for that point. Thus, the "extra" information provided by the bubble plot helps account for data points that might be regarded as outliers or anomalies in a traditional, bivariate scatterplot.

Although the basic idea of a bubble plot is very simple, the resultant graphic is still fairly demanding in terms of the cognitive processing that is required for interpretation. Therefore, it can be difficult to disentangle the patterns among the differently sized points. To provide some guidance for doing so, Figure 4.4 shows some bubble plots created from simulated data; the four panels of the figure represent different kinds of functional dependency between two hypothetical independent variables (designated X_1 and X_2) and one dependent variable (Y).

The first panel (Figure 4.4A) shows a situation similar to that occurring in the electoral college data—two largely uncorrelated independent variables, both exerting separate positive effects on the dependent variable. The relationship between the two variables plotted on the axes of the scatterplot is indicated by the shape of the point cloud (X_1 and Y in this case). The separate effect of the "bubbled" variable (X_2) is signaled by the positions of the differently sized data points. Specifically, larger circles tend to fall near the upper part of the graph and smaller circles fall near the bottom, regardless of their positions along the horizontal axis.

Next, Figure 4.4B shows the situation where only one of the two independent variables has an effect on the dependent variable. In this case, X_1 is correlated with Y and this is, again, shown by the nonrandom, tilted shape of the point cloud. X_2, however, is not related to Y. As a result, there is no discernible pattern in the locations of the differently sized points; large and small circles are interspersed throughout the entire point cloud.

The third panel, Figure 4.4C, shows the same data as Figure 4.4B, but with the roles of the two independent variables reversed. Now, X_2 is shown on the horizontal axis while X_1 is encoded into the bubble sizes. Note that there is no identifiable point cloud within this graph. Instead, plotting symbols are scattered randomly throughout the entire data region. This, of course, reflects the null relationship between the variables plotted on the horizontal and vertical axes. There is, however, a clear, systematic pattern in the *sizes* of the points, with larger circles near the top of the graph and smaller circles near the bottom. This shows, once again, the positive relationship between X_1 and Y.

Finally, Figure 4.4D shows a bubble plot in which the two independent variables both affect the dependent variable. This graph differs from the one shown in the first panel because X_1 and X_2 are highly collinear. In this case, there is a clearly defined shape to the point cloud, stemming from the redundant variability across the two independent variables. In addition, the sizes of the plotting symbols increase smoothly while moving from left to right within the point cloud. This shows that the values of X_2 tend to increase along with the values of X_1. Both the shape of the point cloud and the systematically varying positions of the differently sized circles confirm that the two independent variables are correlated with Y.

36

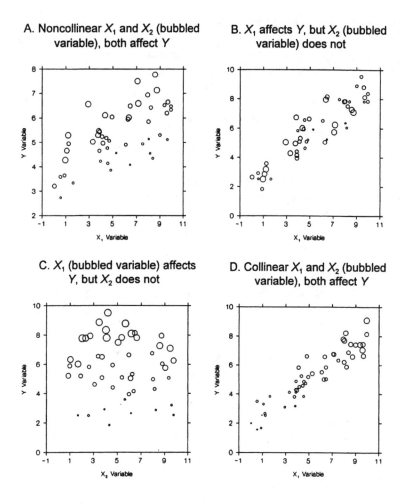

Figure 4.4. Bubble Plot Examples, Using Simulated Data

In summary, a bubble plot requires closer scrutiny than a simple two-dimensional scatterplot, but careful attention to variability in the sizes of the plotted points, as well as to their relative positions, can provide a great deal of useful information about relationships involving three quantitative variables. It is probably easiest to think in terms of three-dimensional space and regard the bubble size as an indicator of depth, along with the height and left-right position, which are indicated by the vertical and horizontal axes, respectively. Thus, the bubble plot could be viewed as a more useful variant of a three-dimensional scatterplot.

The bubble plot has several serious drawbacks that limit its utility for analytic purposes. First, visual detection can be severely inhibited by the overplotting that almost certainly will occur with large datasets. The additional variability introduced by the differing bubble sizes makes it relatively difficult to discern the positions of individual observations within the data region of the graph. When even a few observations are clustered at similar locations, their plotting symbols quickly coalesce into an indistinguishable jumble of overlaid circles.

Overplotting also causes a second problem in bubble plots, by inhibiting visual assembly of the data into systematic patterns. The hypothetical examples shown in Figure 4.4 all involve strong relationships and linear functional forms. With real data, the amount of "noise" often is very large relative to the systematic, structural variability. This will degrade the clarity of any patterns in both the shape of the data point cloud and the sizes of the plotting symbols.

Third, bubble plots entail several problems with visual estimation of data values. The sizes of the plotting symbols show only *relative* differences between observations on the third variable; this is less information than is available about the two variables whose values are shown explicitly on the axes of the plot. Furthermore, if an observation has a large value on the bubbled variable, it may be difficult to determine its precise location relative to the axes. The large diameter of the resultant plotting symbol will span a range of values along either axis. In addition, bubble plots require the analyst to make judgments about the relative sizes of the plotting symbols. It often is not clear to the observer, however, *which* aspect of the size corresponds to the value of the third variable—the diameter or the area of the plotted circle.[13] Regardless of which one it is, judgments about length or area fall at relatively low positions within Cleveland's hierarchy of visual perception tasks.

Conclusions

This chapter has discussed three-dimensional scatterplots and bubble plots as strategies for visualizing trivariate data. In each case, the basic idea is to construct a pictorial representation of the data space. The general advantage of doing so is that the human visual perception system can decode the quantitative information by recognizing the analogy to physical space. The graphical display "translates" an ordered triple of data values for an observation into a small, circular object located somewhere within a box. The two kinds of displays considered in this chapter simply provide differing views of the contents of the box: The three-dimensional scatterplot looks into the box from an oblique perspective, while the bubble plot provides an orthogonal view of one of the box's sides. In either case, the power of the display lies in the fact that the basic information is recognizable, even to someone without training or background in quantitative methods. This undoubtedly is the reason that three-dimensional scatterplots and bubble plots appear frequently in journalistic writing and other presentations aimed at nontechnical audiences. They also are incorporated into virtually all modern graphics software packages, so their prevalence is probably assured well into the future.

The problem is that both three-dimensional scatterplots and bubble plots fall somewhat short as analytical graphics. For the various reasons discussed earlier, these displays do not facilitate the recognition of systematic patterns within data. They also inhibit accurate judgments about the relative magnitudes of data values. These problems are most pronounced in exactly the kinds of situations where graphical displays should provide the strongest advantages over traditional, numerical analyses: Noisy data that conform to relatively complex underlying structures and may contain very large numbers of observations. Furthermore, there is another, obvious limitation: These three-dimensional scatterplots and bubble plots can represent only three variables at a time, even though multivariate analyses frequently incorporate many more sources of variability. The remaining chapters of this monograph will cover a variety of graphical methods that are much less susceptible to these problems and limitations.

5. THE SCATTERPLOT MATRIX

The problems of three-dimensional scatterplots and bubble plots stem from the attempt to simulate visually the exact physical nature of three-dimensional data space. In other words, the use of artistic techniques like oblique views and varying object sizes leads to unacceptable distortions in the visual perception of quantitative information. The basic concept of looking into the data space nevertheless remains intuitively reasonable and conceptually sound. So far, the problems have involved only the operationalization of this idea.

To overcome these limitations, it is necessary to move away from the tools of the representational artist and toward those of technical illustration and drafting. Specifically, let us consider a series of orthogonal views focused on all of the primary directions within the data space. In this context, the term "primary view" refers to a plane formed by two variable axes. The term "orthogonal view" means that the viewing perspective is from a direction perpendicular to a given plane. Combining these two ideas, each orthogonal view is simply a bivariate scatterplot, showing the relationship between two of the variables in the multivariate dataset. With k variables, there are a total of $k(k - 1)$ distinct views, because each pair of variables—X_i and X_j—can be shown in two ways: once with X_i as the horizontal axis variable and X_j on the vertical axis, and again with the two variables' scales shown on the opposite axes within the scatterplot.

Thus, the multivariate data can be shown as a series of bivariate scatterplots (Chambers et al., 1983; Tukey & Tukey, 1981). The number of scatterplots obviously will be very large, relative to the number of variables within the dataset; therefore, it is important that the separate bivariate displays be presented in a way that facilitates overall comprehension and understanding. The scatterplot matrix is intended to accomplish exactly this objective.

Features of the Scatterplot Matrix

A scatterplot matrix is defined as a square, symmetric table or "matrix" of bivariate scatterplots (Cleveland, 1994). This table has k rows and columns, with each one corresponding to a different variable. Each of the table's cells or "panels" formed by the intersection of row i and column j contains the scatterplot showing X_i as the vertical axis variable and X_j as the horizontal axis variable. Because the scatterplot matrix is symmetric about its diagonal, these same variables also appear in panel ji, with their vertical and horizontal positions reversed.

The central feature of the scatterplot matrix is the fact that its off-diagonal panels show all possible bivariate relationships that exist within the multivariate data. This is a deceptively simple, but extremely powerful, strategy for presenting a large amount of information in a systematic and easily understood format. Note also that k is not limited to any particular value, so the scatterplot matrix effectively overcomes the limitations encountered with the trivariate graphical displays considered in the previous chapter.

40

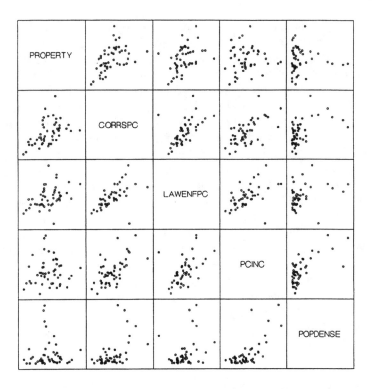

Figure 5.1. Scatterplot Matrix of 1992 State Crime Data

NOTE: PROPERTY = number of property crimes per 100,000 population; CORRSPC = state spending on corrections (dollars per capita); LAWENFPC = state spending on law enforcement (dollars per capita); PCINC = per capita income (thousands of dollars); POPDENSE = population density (thousands per square mile).

Figure 5.1 shows a basic scatterplot matrix, using some data on the American states.[14] The matrix contains 1992 values for five variables. Starting at the top row and moving downward (or from left to right in the columns), the variables and their identifying labels are as follows: The number of property crimes per 100,000 population (PROPERTY), per capita state expenditures on corrections (CORRSPC), per capita state expenditures on law enforcement (LAWENFPC), per capita income (PCINC), and population density (POPDENSE).

Several features of the scatterplot matrix should be emphasized. First, each variable's relationships with all of the other variables are illustrated in the panels contained within a single row or column of the matrix. To accomplish this, the axes within a single row or column all share a common scale. The systematic layout of the variables and the common scales work together to organize the enormous amount of information contained within the scatterplot matrix. In so doing, they enable visual perception of the data's features.

Second, note that the scatterplot matrix presents the data with virtually no embellishment or extra graphical features. Tick marks are omitted from the axes of the panel plots. The scale values are not shown on any of the axes. Each variable's label is shown only once, inside the diagonal cell corresponding to that variable's row and column. The "sparse trimmings" of the scatterplot matrix serve at least two purposes. On one hand, they reduce the physical space used by non-data elements of the display, thereby allowing for larger plot cells or more variables. On the other hand, the lack of extraneous information, along with the shared scale lines in the scatter-plot matrix, focuses the analyst's attention directly onto the most important element of the display—the data themselves. This removes distractions and makes it easier to discern stability and/or variability in the patterns of data points across the cells of the matrix. Of course, this is the overall reason for constructing and using the scatterplot matrix in the first place.

Third, there seems to be some duplication of information built into the scatterplot matrix, because each pair of variables appears in two separate panels of the display—once above the main diagonal, and once again below it. An alternative presentation might try to avoid this redundancy by only including half of the off-diagonal scatterplot panels. An example of this is shown in Figure 5.2, which presents the lower-left triangle (and the labeled diagonal panels) from the original scatterplot matrix. In fact, this type of display was the first form of scatterplot matrix to appear in the literature, and it is usually called a *draftsman's display* to distinguish it from the square version (e.g., Chambers et al., 1983).

This "half-matrix" version produces a somewhat more compact display than the full scatterplot matrix. One could argue that it maximizes the data-ink ratio and saves space. The half-matrix presentation, however, almost certainly inhibits accurate and easy visual processing of the data. For one thing, with a full square scatterplot matrix, it is necessary to scan only across one row, or down one column, of the display to examine a single variable's relationships with all the other variables. In the half-matrix version, the viewer must "turn a visual corner" when examining all vari-ables except for those in the first column or last row of the display. When this occurs, the scale for the variable under investigation will appear on the vertical axis in some cells and the horizontal axis in others.

42

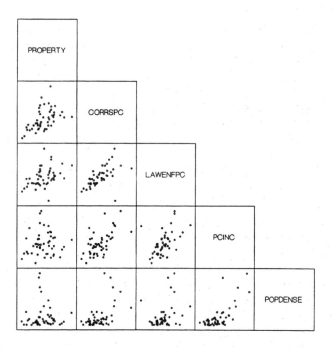

Figure 5.2. Lower Triangular Version of Scatterplot Matrix, 1992 State Crime Data

NOTE: PROPERTY = number of property crimes per 100,000 population; CORRSPC = state spending on corrections (dollars per capita); LAWENFPC = state spending on law enforcement (dollars per capita); PCINC = per capita income (thousands of dollars); POPDENSE = population density (thousands per square mile).

Another problem with the half-matrix display is that the upper and lower triangles of the full matrix do not really show exactly the same information; instead, they contain transposed versions of the pairwise scatterplots. This is important because visual processing may well be influenced by the row and column placements of the two variables in any bivariate display; in other words, it may be easier to discern features like outliers and functional dependencies when a given variable is on the vertical axis, rather than the horizontal, and vice versa. For reasons like these, the half-matrix version of the scatterplot matrix almost certainly reduces the effectiveness of the display; therefore, it generally should be avoided in favor of the full, square version.

Variations of the Scatterplot Matrix

The basic scatterplot matrix can be varied and enhanced in many ways. One relatively minor modification is to change the orientation of the main diagonal in the display. Although this does not have much effect on the visual impression to be gained from the display, it does have important implications for the coordinate system that is used to refer to the separate panels within the matrix. Up to this point, the contents of the scatterplot matrix have reflected standard practice in numerical matrices and tables. That is, the main diagonal runs from upper left to lower right and the panels are indexed by double subscripts in which the first value indicates the row and the second value indicates the column. According to this system, $panel_{ij}$ refers to the bivariate scatterplot shown at the intersection of the ith row (counting from the top) and the jth column (counting from the left). In Figure 5.1, for example, $panel_{12}$ shows the scatterplot with property crime rates on the vertical axis (i.e., the variable in the first row of the matrix) and corrections expenditures on the horizontal axis (i.e., the variable in the second column of the matrix).

There is certainly nothing wrong with the previous arrangement, but another system seems to be more consistent with general design considerations in graphical displays of quantitative information. Figure 5.3 shows the state data arranged according to this alternative scheme. A glance at the figure reveals that there is only one change in the physical layout of the display: The main diagonal now runs from lower left to upper right. This relatively minor alteration is accompanied by a corresponding change in the coordinate system. Now, each panel is designated by an ordered pair of values, say (i, j). The first value in the ordered pair refers to the panel's *column* and the second value to its *row*; note that this is exactly the opposite from the usual cell notation for numeric matrices. Furthermore, the numbering system for the rows and columns now begins in the lower-left corner panel. In Figure 5.3, the panel at position (2, 1) refers to the scatterplot in the second column (from the left) of the bottom row, showing crime rates on the vertical axis, plotted against corrections spending on the horizontal axis. Similarly, panel (4, 5) designates the scatterplot with population density as the vertical axis variable and per capita income on the horizontal axis.

Of course, the specific coordinate system employed in the scatterplot matrix is completely arbitrary, so the new version is just as legitimate as the original method for designating plotting panels. It will, however, undoubtedly cause some confusion among readers who are already familiar and comfortable with traditional numeric matrix cell notation. Cleveland

44

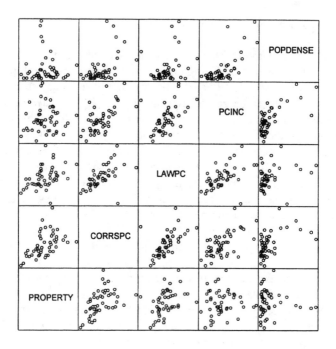

Figure 5.3. Scatterplot Matrix of 1992 State Crime Data, Constructed Using Graphical Coordinate System*

*Each panel is identified by an ordered pair of values, such as (i, j), which designates the ith column and the jth row of the scatterplot matrix. The values of the indices start with 1 for the lower-left corner panel; they increase from left to right within rows, and from bottom to top within columns.

NOTE: PROPERTY = number of property crimes per 100,000 population; CORRSPC = state spending on corrections (dollars per capita); LAWENFPC = state spending on law enforcement (dollars per capita); PCINC = per capita income (thousands of dollars); POPDENSE = population density (thousands per square mile).

(1993b) argues that this new notation actually is more consistent with general graphical practice and notation. That is, most two-dimensional graphs place the origin in the lower left-hand corner. Similarly, position within a graph is indicated using an ordered pair of values, say (x, y), where x refers to the abscissa (i.e., position along the horizontal axis) and y refers to the ordinate (i.e., position along the vertical axis). Therefore, a similar coordinate system seems to be appropriate for positioning the components of multipanel graphical displays, such as the scatterplot matrices considered in the remainder of this chapter and the conditioning plots presented in the next chapter.

A second possible enhancement involves the contents of the diagonal cells in the scatterplot matrix. Up to this point, these cells have been left completely empty, except for the variable labels. This is done deliberately, to avoid any extraneous features that might interfere with visual scanning across an entire row or column of the matrix. Still, this does leave some unused space within the graphical display. One useful addition to the scatterplot matrix places information about the univariate distributions within these otherwise "wasted" panels. Any of the available univariate graphics could be used; however, box plots are particularly well suited for this purpose. They take up little room in the panel (so the variable label can still be included without too much crowding), they are not subject to distortions based upon bin- or bandwidths (which would affect histograms and smoothed density plots), and they are visually distinct from the scatterplots contained in the off-diagonal panels (unlike univariate scatterplots or quantile plots). For all these reasons, box plots in the diagonal cells of a scatterplot matrix are a particularly useful way to provide univariate information about the individual variables.

Figure 5.4 shows a scatterplot matrix of the state data with box plots added to the display. Most of the univariate distributions seem to be quite well behaved (i.e., symmetric, with few outliers). The one serious exception to this is population density, which has a distribution that is severely skewed toward large values. Of course, this same information could have been gleaned from careful inspection of the off-diagonal cells. The univariate box plot, however, shows this feature with unmistakable clarity. In any event, the skewness suggests that it might be useful to transform this variable's values. Accordingly, the remaining displays of these data will employ logged values of population density, which produce a much more symmetric distribution. This variable is labeled LOG.PD in subsequent displays.

A third enhancement places a smooth curve within the off-diagonal cells of the scatterplot matrix. Within each display panel, the smooth curve traces the central tendency of the conditional distribution on the vertical axis variable across the range of values on the horizontal axis variable. The objective is to summarize any pairwise functional dependencies that may exist within the data. Any scatterplot smoother can be used for this purpose, but there are two that appear most frequently in practice. First, the ordinary least square (OLS) regression line provides a parametric fit, when the analyst is willing to make prior assumptions about the functional form of the interrelationships among the variables. Second, a loess curve is a convenient strategy for fitting a nonparametric smooth curve, thereby allowing "the data to speak for themselves." In either case, the smooth

46

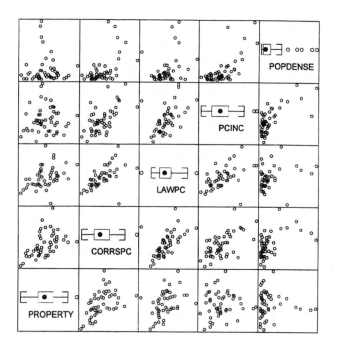

Figure 5.4. Scatterplot Matrix of 1992 State Crime Data, Box and Whisker Diagrams Included on the Main Diagonal

NOTE: PROPERTY = number of property crimes per 100,000 population; CORRSPC = state spending on corrections (dollars per capita); LAWENFPC = state spending on law enforcement (dollars per capita); PCINC = per capita income (thousands of dollars); POPDENSE = population density (thousands per square mile).

curve within each display panel summarizes the central tendency of the conditional distributions on the vertical axis variable across the range of values on the horizontal axis variable.

Figure 5.5 shows the state data again, with loess curves added to the off-diagonal panels. This figure shows another good reason for using the full, square scatterplot matrix, rather than a half-matrix, lower diagonal version: Functional dependence is an asymmetric phenomenon. The smooth curve for a pair of variables will differ when one or the other variable is placed on the vertical (or horizontal) axis. For example, consider the relationship between law enforcement expenditures and property crime rates. Panel (3, 1) shows a relatively complicated nonlinear curve when expenditures are on the horizontal axis and crime rates are on the vertical

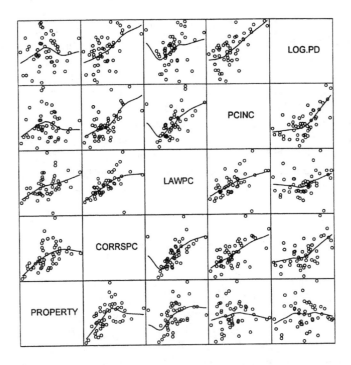

Figure 5.5. Scatterplot Matrix of 1992 State Crime Data, Nonparametric Loess Smooth Curves Fitted to Bivariate Data in Off-Diagonal Panels*

*The loess curves are fitted using locally linear fitting (i.e., $\lambda = 1$) and a smoothing parameter (α) set equal to 0.75. Robustness iterations are not used.
NOTE: PROPERTY = number of property crimes per 100,000 population; CORRSPC = state spending on corrections (dollars per capita); LAWENFPC = state spending on law enforcement (dollars per capita); PCINC = per capita income (thousands of dollars); LOG.PD = $\log_{10}$ population density ($\log_{10}$ thousands per square mile).

axis. Panel (1, 3)—which contains the same variables, with their axis positions reversed—shows a nearly linear relationship. Thus, one would reach different conclusions about the structure within the data from the corresponding panels above and below the main diagonal. For this reason, it is important to show both of them within the display, to provide the "full picture" to the analyst.

In principle, any of the enhancements available for bivariate scatterplots also could be used in a scatterplot matrix. Similarly, several different enhancements could be used at the same time, to maximize the overall amount of information within the display. In practice, however, this can be somewhat problematic. The smaller size of the individual plots in the panels of the matrix necessarily reduces visual resolution of the graphical information. Added features in the display tend to produce a "cluttered" look. They could easily overshadow elements of the data, thereby violating the perceptual objectives of detection, assembly, and estimation. For this reason, enhancements for scatterplot matrices should be used sparingly. It is better to produce several displays of the same data, each of which contains a single enhancement (e.g., univariate distributions in one, smooth curves in another, and so on), instead of a single display that tries to show all the data and summarize all their salient features at the same time.

Using and Interpreting the Scatterplot Matrix

The scatterplot matrix provides a fairly comprehensive view of the data. In fact, the sheer amount of information can make the display difficult to comprehend without a relatively systematic strategy to guide the investigation. Any attempt to extract information from a scatterplot matrix, therefore, should proceed by capitalizing on its distinctive features: the systematic layout and the shared axes of the display panels. The overall procedure usually involves scanning across panels within single rows and/or columns of the scatterplot matrix to discern regularities and distinctive features in the data. We can use the state data and the displays already presented in this chapter to show how this might work in a specific research context.

The initial examination probably should be aimed at discerning problematic features of the data. For this purpose, it is best to use a basic, unadorned version of the scatterplot matrix, such as that shown in Figure 5.1. A glance back at that display reveals a visually prominent feature in the panels of the rightmost column and the bottom row: Most of the data points are squeezed into a small portion of the panels in these dimensions of the matrix. Obviously, these panels all involve the same variable—population density. The common source of these unusual bivariate displays immediately suggests that it might be useful to examine the univariate distribution for this variable more closely. This leads to the addition of the box plots in the main diagonal, an enhancement that was shown in Figure 5.4. As explained earlier, the box plot clearly reveals the severe skewness in the population density variable.

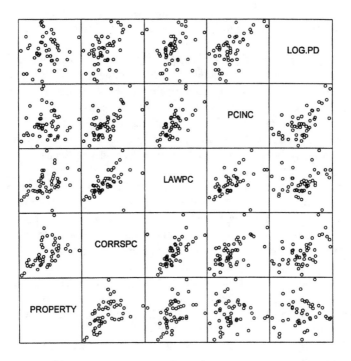

Figure 5.6. Basic Scatterplot Matrix of 1992 State Crime Data (including log population density)

NOTE: PROPERTY = number of property crimes per 100,000 population; CORRSPC = state spending on corrections (dollars per capita); LAWENFPC = state spending on law enforcement (dollars per capita); PCINC = per capita income (thousands of dollars); LOG.PD = $\log_{10}$ population density ($\log_{10}$ thousands per square mile).

Figure 5.6 shows a version of the basic scatterplot matrix that has been modified to take the preceding distributional information into account. The display contains the same information as Figure 5.1, except it shows logged values of population density. The main diagonal of the matrix also has been reversed, as discussed above. A glance at the top row and the rightmost column shows that the data points are now spread more evenly throughout the display panels involving population density. Although the univariate distributions are not shown in this display, the transformation of the latter variable has led successfully to a more nearly symmetric distribution.

After addressing any glaring problems in the data, the next step is to examine the display for interesting patterns and structure. Several authors have pointed out that the scatterplot matrix is a graphical analog to the correlation or covariance matrix in that it conveys information about all possible bivariate relationships among the variables. As with the simple scatterplot, however, the graphical display has an important advantage over its numerical counterpart: It shows all the data, rather than simply summarizing how well the data conform to one particular kind of structure (e.g., linearity in the case of the correlation/covariance matrix).

The scatterplot matrix in Figure 5.6 immediately reveals a great deal of information about the interrelationships among these variables. Although there are many interesting features in these data, let us focus particular attention on the panels involving the property crime rate. Scanning across the bottom row in the matrix, it is readily apparent that rates of property crime are positively related to state expenditures on both corrections and law enforcement; this is signaled by the clear lower-left to upper-right "tilts" in the respective point clouds. There does not seem to be any clear structure involving either per capita income or logged population density.

It also is important to examine the shapes of the point clouds within the panels of the scatterplot matrix, to gain insights about the nature of any interrelationships among the variables. For example, several of the point clouds seem to exhibit a sort of "diagonal fan shape," in which the width of the fan changes along with the values of the horizontal axis variable. This pattern seems to be especially prominent in panels (1, 2) and (4, 5), although it is also visible elsewhere. From panel (1, 2), it appears that, as property crime rates increase, the *variability* in corrections expenditure levels increases, along with the central tendency of the latter variable. In panel (4, 5), the fan-shaped pattern is oriented in the opposite direction; in other words, vertical variance *decreases* from left to right along the horizontal axis. This indicates that states with low income levels show higher variance in their log population densities than do states with larger per capita income values. The latter all have fairly uniform, high log population densities. The substantive implications of these patterns are unclear, but they could indicate sources of heteroskedasticity that should be taken into account in any subsequent statistical models that might be fitted to these data.

The scatterplot matrix also can be used to gain information about the functional forms of relationships among the variables. Some of the panels clearly exhibit linear dependencies, such as panel (4, 5) showing the relationship between per capita income and log population densities. Others seem to be nonlinear, such as panel (2, 1), which shows how property crime rates vary across levels of state corrections expenditures. Visual assessment of functional forms is a difficult and highly subjective process whenever there is anything more than minimal noise in the data, so it usually is helpful to add fit scatterplot smoothers to the panels of the scatterplot matrix, as was done in Figure 5.5. The loess curves shown in that display confirm most of the visual impressions already mentioned, and they also reveal some other features, such as the "check mark" or "hockey stick" patterns that appear within the scatterplots in the third column. All of this information contributes to the analyst's understanding of the structure underlying the empirical observations.

The scatterplot matrix also can be used to identify unusual observations within the data. For one thing, there are a number of outliers evident in the panels. In fact, the "check mark" pattern mentioned above may be the result of a single observation that appears near the leftmost extreme of all panels in the third column of the matrix—a state with very low levels of spending on law enforcement and unusually large values on all of the other variables. Similarly, there is a single outlier that appears in row two (from the bottom) of the matrix, indicating a state that has unusually high corrections expenditures, even though it also shows moderate to high values on all of the other variables. Identifying outliers like these is important, both for intrinsic purposes (i.e., What is it that makes these states unusual? Are there coding errors in their data values?) and also because they can have a particularly strong effect on parameter estimates in any statistical models that may be fit to the data. In fact, it may be useful to eliminate some of these isolated data points and reconstruct the display, to see what effect the outliers have on the estimated bivariate structures.

The discussion in this section has shown how an analyst might use a scatterplot matrix to examine a set of multivariate data. The steps outlined above are suggestive, rather than definitive. They would have to be adjusted to the requirements, objectives, and limitations of any other data analysis context. The basic components of the process, however, probably would remain very similar to those outlined here. Generally, the process would involve an iterative series of graphing and fitting steps aimed at (a) exposing the basic contents of the data, (b) imposing overall structures on the data, and (c) identifying observations that do not conform to the more general patterns that exist within the data. Of course, these steps are common to all forms of statistical modeling and data analysis—numerical approaches, as well as graphical. The scatterplot matrix, however, facilitates this process by imposing a regular organization on the data themselves. This makes it much easier for the analyst to look at the enormous amount of information that may be shown within the display, comprehend its content, and discern the interesting patterns and features contained therein.

Conclusions

The scatterplot matrix conveys a large amount of information in a very succinct and efficient manner. The careful and regular layout of the axes avoids the arbitrariness encountered with the icon plots discussed in Chapters 2 and 3. The orthogonal views within the panels and the generally expandable size of the matrix (i.e., to $k > 3$ dimensions) also overcome the limitations encountered with the trivariate graphical displays considered in Chapter 4 (i.e., oblique views of only three variables at a time). The importance of the scatterplot matrix as a graphical depiction of multivariate data is probably best indicated by Cleveland's (1994) comment that "An award should be given for (its) invention" (p. 193).

It is, perhaps, tempting to think about the scatterplot matrix as a series of bivariate graphical displays; however, it is important to emphasize that its primary purpose is to show *multivariate* data. In fact, the scatterplot matrix—a two-dimensional display in physical terms—is a flattened representation of the full data space, which is multidimensional, at least in conceptual terms. The "translation" from the latter to the former is analogous to (but much simpler than) the Mercator projections used to create a flat map representing the surface features of a three-dimensional sphere.

The scatterplot matrix does have two potential disadvantages. First, this kind of graphical display (like most others) is effectively limited to small numbers of variables. As k increases, so does the number of panels in the matrix. Given the limited size of the plotting region in most display media, the size of each panel must be reduced accordingly. At some point, visual resolution of the point clouds within the panels will be degraded to an unacceptable degree.

Second, the scatterplot matrix graphs multivariate *data*, but it cannot really show multivariate *structure*, because the scatterplot within each panel is constructed completely independently of the information in any other panel. Somewhat ironically, the problem is that each variable is usually correlated with more than one other variable. Whenever this occurs, the data point locations in any given panel will be affected by their positions within the other panels. This is exactly why multivariate data are interesting in the first place: Researchers usually want to see how *several* variables interact with one another, simultaneously. This simply cannot be accomplished when a scatterplot matrix is used to display the data.[15]

In graphical terms, each panel of the scatterplot matrix shows point locations on only one single plane within the k-dimensional data space. The panels make no attempt to represent variability that may occur simultaneously along other directions within the space. The scatterplot matrix also shows only a limited and rigidly defined set of directions within the data space, that is, the directions defined strictly by the variable axes. The methods to be considered in the next two chapters provide more flexibility with respect to the view of the multidimensional data space that is depicted on the two-dimensional display medium.

6. CONDITIONING PLOTS

When confronted with multivariate *data*, researchers usually are interested in multivariate *structure*; that is, nonrandom patterns of observations that involve several variables simultaneously. As we have seen, it is a major challenge to produce effective graphical representations for this kind of information. Some methods are too heavily based on subjective decisions on the part of the analyst (e.g., iconic displays), other methods are problematic for graphical perception (three-dimensional plots), and still other methods break the multivariate data down into a series of strictly bivariate displays (scatterplot matrices). This chapter will discuss *conditioning plots*, a graphical display strategy that attempts explicitly to overcome all the previous limitations.

The basic purpose of the conditioning plot is to show how a dependent variable is affected by several other variables, simultaneously—hence, it addresses the problem of multivariate structure, mentioned above. The method used to do this is elegant in its simplicity, and it relies on one of the most fundamental concepts of research design. A conditioning plot shows the bivariate relationship between two variables (say, X and Y), while holding constant (or "conditioning upon") the values of one or more other variables (say, X_3 through X_k).

There are (at least potentially) many different kinds of conditioning plots. This chapter will consider three types: casement displays, coplots, and trellis displays. All three of these graphs can be employed to display the same kind of information. The differences between them lie only in the details.

Basic Features and Definitions

Regardless of specific type, a conditioning plot is always a multipanel display, constructed as follows. First, the values of each conditioning variable are divided into a series of m intervals or *slices*. Then, each slice of the conditioning variable (or combination of slices, if there is more than one conditioning variable) is allocated to one of m separate panels in the conditioning plot. The panel itself typically shows the bivariate scatterplot for the two remaining variables, X and Y. Each panel of the conditioning plot controls "physically" for the conditioning variables, by only including the data points that fall within the slice corresponding to that panel.

Following Cleveland's (1993b) terminology, the variable that corresponds to the vertical axis in each display panel of the conditioning plot is called the "dependent variable," as usual. The variable that is shown on the horizontal axis of each panel is called the "panel variable." Not surprisingly, the sliced variable that is used to create the panels is called the "conditioning variable."

The panels of the conditioning plot are always laid out in a rectangular array, and specific panels are identified using the graphical coordinate system introduced in the last chapter. In other words, panel (1, 1) lies in the lower left corner of the display, and it represents the slice with the smallest values of the conditioning variable. Panel (2, 1) is the second panel from the left in the first (or bottom) row, and it contains the second-smallest interval of values on the conditioning variable. The panels proceed in this manner, from left to right within rows, and from the bottom row upward, if more than one row is necessary in the display.

One of the most crucial features of any conditioning plot is the regularity in the displays across the conditioning panels. Tufte (1983) calls this the principle of "small multiples." This term simply means that the scale rectangles and other graphical "trimmings" of the scatterplots remain fixed across the panels. The *only* thing that changes are the data themselves. The panels of the conditioning plot are, therefore, analogous to the frames in a strip of a movie film that depict movement by passing quickly in front of the viewer. With a conditioning plot, the analyst scans across the panels and observes how the data "move," relative to the fixed references of the scale rectangles.

The Casement Display

Let us begin with a fairly simple example of a conditioning plot: a trivariate structure consisting of a functional relationship between two continuous variables, controlling for the values of a discrete, nominal variable. This example also will illustrate a common reason for using a conditioning plot: explicating a complex and/or unexpected pattern in bivariate data.

Figure 6.1 shows a scatterplot of logged 1986 state spending on AFDC (Aid to Families With Dependent Children, a welfare program) and state poverty rates.[16] A loess curve has been fitted to the data, and the aspect ratio has been set to a value of 2, to bank the smooth curve to an orientation relatively close to 45 degrees. This produces a rather tall and narrow display, but it also optimizes visual perception of variability in the local slopes of the fitted curve.

The most striking aspect of Figure 6.1 is the markedly nonlinear and complex functional dependence of logged AFDC expenditures on poverty rates. In states with relatively low poverty levels (below a value of about 14 on the horizontal axis), the two variables show a generally positive relationship. Even within this region of the scatterplot, however, the curve is nonmonotonic, dipping slightly downward around a value of 12 or 13 on the horizontal axis. Among states with higher poverty rates, the overall relationship changes direction, so that increasing numbers of poor people correspond to sharply lower levels of AFDC spending. Once again, there is a slight reversal in the curve, which begins to slope upward at the extreme right side of the scatterplot.

One possible explanation for the nonlinear, nonmonotone functional dependency in Figure 6.1 is that there are regional differences in the ways that the American states provide for their poor citizens. This hypothesis can be investigated very easily, using a conditioning plot, such as that shown in Figure 6.2. The display has four panels. Each panel shows the scatterplot between log AFDC expenditures and poverty rates for the states that fall within one of four regions: Northeast, West, Midwest, and South. Thus, the dependent variable in this plot is log AFDC spending, the panel variable is state poverty rate, and the conditioning variable is region. Once again, loess curves have been fitted to the data to facilitate visual interpretation of the functional relationships. Note, however, that the smooth curves are fit separately to the data within each category of the regional conditioning variable. Therefore, the placement and shape of the curve in any panel of the conditioning plot will not affect, nor will it be affected by, the curves in any of the other panels.

The dependence panels in Figure 6.2 represent a set of nominal categories; nevertheless, they are placed in a systematic ordering from left to right within the conditioning plot. Specifically, the four regions are ordered according to their median poverty rates.[17] This makes it much easier to see how the conditioned scatterplots between the panel and

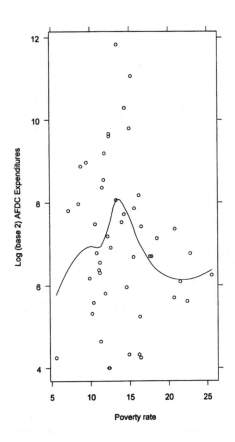

Figure 6.1. Scatterplot of 1986 State AFDC Expenditure (in log $1,000s) and State Poverty Rate (percentages)

NOTE: Loess curves in panels are based on locally quadratic fitting ($\lambda = 2$), smoothing parameter (α) set equal to 0.75, and robustness iterations.

dependent variables correspond to "piecewise" components of the original relationship.

The variation across the regions is immediately obvious in Figure 6.2. If the separate panels from the conditioning plot were placed on top of one another, the superimposed, region-specific loess curves would correspond fairly closely to the loess curve that was shown in the original, bivariate scatterplot. Thus, the functional form of the relationship between welfare spending and poverty levels varies markedly across the regions, and this

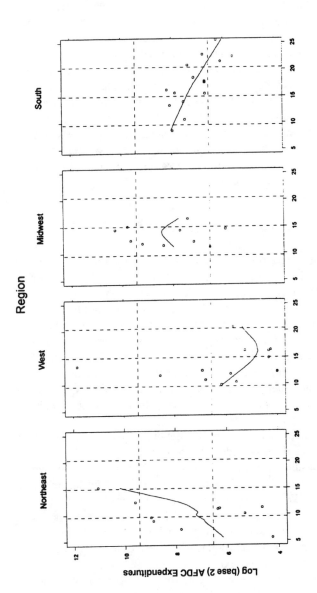

Figure 6.2. Casement Plot Showing 1986 State AFDC Expenditures Versus Poverty Rate, Controlling for Region

NOTE: Loess curves in panels are based on locally linear fitting (1 = 1), smoothing parameter (a) set equal to 1, and robustness iterations.

seems to account for the markedly nonlinear functional dependence shown in Figure 6.1. For present purposes, the important point is that the conditioning plot provides an immediate and striking insight about a bivariate relationship that seems complex and rather puzzling at first glance.

The type of conditioning plot shown in Figure 6.2 has been called a *casement display* because "it is like cranking open a series of casement windows (into the data space), drawing each data point to the nearest window, and then cranking them shut again (Chambers et al., 1983, p. 141). The casement display is the simplest conditioning plot. It is merely an array of juxtaposed but separate scatterplots, each of which shows the subset of the overall data corresponding to the observations that fall within a single category of the conditioning variable.

Conditioning on Values of a Continuous Variable

The conditioning plot shown in Figure 6.2 is particularly simple in that it involves a single conditioning variable, and the latter divides the data into a small number of discrete categories. In fact, conditioning plots can be generalized very easily to deal with more complicated multivariate data situations. Consider a quantitative conditioning variable with values that range in a relatively continuous manner across some interval. It usually is impossible to use conditioning panels corresponding to the distinct values of such a variable: Being continuous, there may be almost as many distinct values of the conditioning variable as there are data points. Quantitative variables therefore must be *sliced* into intervals to use them for conditioning purposes.

The resultant slices themselves must meet two requirements. First, they must be wide enough to provide reliable estimates of the conditioned, bivariate relationship. Excessively narrow conditioning intervals would contain too few observations. When this occurs, noise in the data (emanating from factors like measurement errors, model misspecifications, and general stochastic factors) can make it difficult to observe systematic patterns. The slices of the conditioning variable therefore must contain a sufficiently large number of data points to enable the analyst to discern any underlying structures that may exist.

Second, the slicing intervals must be narrow enough to allow the analyst to observe any changes in the bivariate structure that occur across the range of the conditioning variable. In other words, slices that are too wide may improperly combine distinct subsets of observations that conform to different underlying structures. If so, then the panels of the coplot would exhibit distorted patterns in the data points.

It often is impossible to meet both of the preceding criteria using slices that divide the data points into mutually exclusive subsets. The solution to this problem is simple, but somewhat unusual: Slice the conditioning variable into *overlapping* intervals. This allows for a sizable number of slices but still places a sufficient number of observations into each slice.

The use of overlapping slices does not violate the integrity of the data in any way. The objective of the coplot is to provide a "moving window" on a bivariate relationship. This movement takes place across the range of the conditioning variable's values. As the window moves across the scale of values, new data points are continuously coming into view on one side of the window, and others are moving out of view on the other side of the window. The separate panels of the coplot provide "snapshots" of the results from this continuous movement. If the snapshots are taken relatively close together (which they must be, to avoid missing any of the data), it is inevitable that certain points will show up in more than one panel. Thus, the use of overlapping slices provides an effective and parsimonious solution to the problems posed by continuous conditioning variables.

The boundaries of the slices used for the conditioning intervals are relatively arbitrary. Generally speaking, datasets with smaller numbers of observations will require wider intervals. Beyond this, there are no clear-cut rules. Experience suggests that, within reason, the particular selection of slices will have little effect on the information that is obtained from the coplot (Chambers et al., 1983).

Cleveland (1993b) recommends defining the slices so that they all contain the same proportion of data points, and that the amount of overlap between adjacent slices is constant. This can be accomplished using the *equal-count* algorithm. To use this procedure, the n observations on the conditioning variable, say X, are sorted, resulting in the ordered array of values, $x_{[1]}, x_{[2]}, \ldots, x_{[n]}$. Then, the desired number of slices, m, is specified, along with the fraction of observations to be shared by adjacent slices, f. This information is used to calculate the number of values that falls within each sliced interval (called r) as follows:

(6.1)
$$r = \frac{n}{m(1-f)+f}$$

Finally, the preceding information is used to calculate the lower and upper endpoints of the qth slice (called l_q and u_q, respectively) as follows:

(6.2a)
$$l_q = x_{[1] + (q - 1)(1 - f)r}$$

(6.2b)
$$u_q = x_{[r] + (q - 1)(1 - f)r}$$

Note that Equation 6.1 will generally produce a noninteger value for r; similarly, the subscripts in Equations 6.2a and 6.2b usually will evaluate to fractional results. When this occurs, the latter are simply rounded to integers, to obtain the indices of the slice endpoints. With most empirical datasets, the rounding makes it impossible to meet exactly the objectives of the equal count algorithm, but the final slices will all still have *approximately* the same number of observations and *approximately* the same proportion of members shared with their respective neighboring slices.

To illustrate the use of a conditioning plot with a continuous conditioning variable, we will go back to the data on 1992 state crime rates that were introduced in the previous chapter. Specifically, each state's property crime rate will be viewed as a function of its law enforcement spending, while controlling for per capita income.

The first step is to slice the per capita income variable into a set of conditioning intervals. The total number of observations is relatively small, at $n = 48$. To accommodate this, we will use $m = 6$ slices—a fairly large number, given the size of the dataset—but allow 75% overlap ($f = 0.75$) between adjacent slices. Applying Equation 6.1 to these figures produces an r value of 21.33; hence, the number of data points within each slice will be about 21. The endpoints of the slices are determined by applying Equations 6.2a and 6.2b for values of q ranging from 1 to 6 (the specified value of m) and rounding the results to integer subscript values. The resultant endpoints are as follows: The first slice ranges from $x_{[1]}$ to $x_{[21]}$, the second slice contains $x_{[6]}$ through $x_{[27]}$, the third slice contains $x_{[12]}$ through $x_{[32]}$, the fourth slice contains $x_{[17]}$ through $x_{[37]}$, the fifth slice contains $x_{[22]}$ through $x_{[43]}$, and the sixth slice ranges from $x_{[28]}$ to the final observation, $x_{[48]}$. Thus, the second and fifth slices each contain 22 observations, while all the others contain 21 observations apiece.

The Coplot Display

Figure 6.3 shows a conditioning plot in which property crime rate is the dependent variable, per capita law enforcement spending is the panel

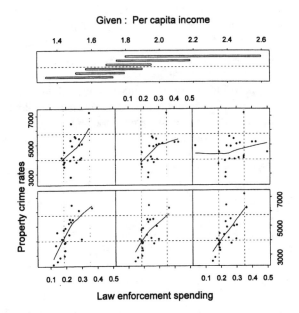

Figure 6.3. Coplot of 1992 Property Crime Rates Versus Law Enforcement Spending, Conditioned on Per Capita Income

variable, and per capita income is the sliced conditioning variable. This type of display is called a *coplot* (Cleveland, 1993b). The distinctive feature is that the overall graphical display is divided into two parts: First, the *given panel* shown at the top of the display provides a graphical representation of the conditioning slices. The horizontal axis in this panel corresponds to the range of values on the conditioning variable, and the horizontal bars show the slices themselves. Once again, the number of data points within each slice is approximately constant, but the widths of the slices vary inversely with the local density in the conditioning variable's distribution. The second part of the coplot consists of the six *dependence panels*. They are laid out in the lower part of the display, and they show the bivariate relationship between the dependent variable and the panel variable for the observations that fall within each of the conditioning slices.

Several features of the coplot display method facilitate visual processing. First, the layout of the information in the given panel reflects the layout of the dependence panels. In both sections of the graph, conditioning intervals begin in the lower left, and they increase while moving from left to right, and upward from one row to the next. The dotted line in the given panel also emphasizes the location of the break between the two rows in the dependence panels. Thus, it is very easy to see which part of the data is shown within each panel of the display.

Second, there are no graphical features that fall in between adjacent dependence panels within the display. This ensures that there are no visual interruptions encountered while scanning from one panel to the next. This should, in turn, make it easier to recognize any changes in the functional relationship between the variables that may occur across the successive conditioning intervals.

Third, smooth curves have been fitted to the point clouds within the coplot. Their purpose is to summarize the functional dependence that occurs within each panel, and therefore to make obvious any changes that exist from one panel to the next. To do so, the curves are fitted separately to the data points within the respective dependence panels. In this case, the nonparametric loess smoother is used, because we are taking a relatively exploratory perspective on the data. Any other smoothing algorithm could be used as well. For example, if the point clouds within the panels conform to linear shapes, it might be helpful to fit an OLS regression line to the data. Although the fitting criterion is a bit more stringent than with loess, the regression approach has the advantage of generating models of the data that can more easily be expressed in numerical form (i.e., the regression equations for the bivariate linear fits in the respective dependence panels).

The information presented in Figure 6.3 immediately indicates the presence of an interaction between law enforcement spending and per capita income. Specifically, the functional relationship is positive, nearly linear, and quite strong within the first four dependence panels (that is, the three in the bottom row, and the leftmost panel in the top row). This shows that, in states with moderate to low per capita incomes, relatively small differences in law enforcement spending levels coincide with quite large differences (in the same direction) in property crime rates. This situation changes among states with higher per capita incomes. The orientations of the loess curves in dependence panels (2, 2) and (3, 2) are still predominantly positive; however, their general slopes are much shallower than those in the first four panels. Apparently, the connection between law enforcement spending and property crime rates is much weaker for states with relatively high per capita incomes.

Along with the interaction, there is another interesting feature that can be discerned in Figure 6.3. Looking across the successive dependence panels, the general heights of the point clouds do not change very much. The dashed grid lines shown within the panels are very helpful for seeing that this is the case. In every panel, all but a few stray observations fall below the upper horizontal grid line; the vast majority of the data points shown in the coplot fall within the lower two-thirds of the respective dependence panels. Thus, the overall *amount* of property crime does not change very much across levels of per capita income, even though the former variable's *relationship* with law enforcement spending does vary across the same income strata within the dataset.

In summary, the coplot shown in Figure 6.3 shows an enormous amount of information about the structure within this particular set of data. Clearly, property crime rates should not be viewed as a simple linear function of law enforcement spending. Instead, any specification of functional form would have to take the interaction between law enforcement spending and per capita income into account, to obtain an accurate depiction of the underlying structure. For now, though, the important point is that we are able to learn a great deal simply by looking at a visual representation of the multivariate data.

The Trellis Display Strategy

The newest and potentially most powerful form of conditioning plot is called a *trellis display* (Becker et al., 1995). Once again, the objective is to show conditional dependence, or how the nature of a bivariate relationship changes while controlling for one or more other variables. Physically, the layout of a trellis display is similar to that of a coplot; however, it contains only dependence panels—there is no separate given panel. Instead, the information about the conditioning slices is now conveyed by the contents of a strip label that is included at the top of each dependence panel. The term "trellis display" arises because the resultant rectangular array of dependence panels is somewhat reminiscent of a garden trellis.

Figure 6.4 presents an example of a trellis display, using the state-level presidential voting data that were introduced in Chapter 3. Specifically, the figure shows the relationship between Clinton vote percentages and the partisanship of state electorates, conditioned upon electorate ideologies. The conditioning variable is divided into four slices, with 75% overlap between adjacent slices. Applying Equation 6.1 to the values of $n = 48$ (the number of states in the dataset), $m = 4$ (the desired number of conditioning intervals), and $f = 0.75$ (the desired amount of overlap), there are approximately 27 observations contained within each slice.

Note how the information about the conditioning intervals is incorporated directly into the trellis display. At the top of each given panel, there

64

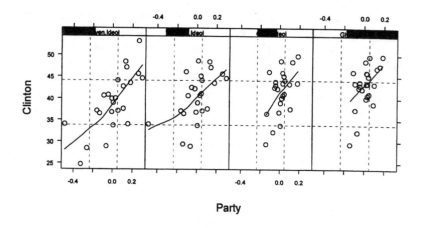

Figure 6.4. Trellis Display of 1992 State Vote Percentage for Clinton Versus Electorate Partisanship, Conditioning on Electorate Ideology

is a labeled strip containing a shaded rectangle. The label shows the name of the conditioning variable. The width of the strip in each panel represents the full range of values on the conditioning variable. The shaded rectangle indicates the slice of the conditioning variable that is shown in that particular given panel. The position of the shaded rectangle shows the relative location of the conditioning interval within the conditioning variable's range, while the size of the slice indicates the relative width of each interval. Thus, the strip labels now contain all the information that previously was presented in the separate given panel of a coplot.

Like the previous examples, Figure 6.4 shows loess curves in the given panels. The aspect ratio of the overall display has been determined by banking to 45 degrees. Note that even though the loess curves are fitted separately to the data points in the respective panels, the banking process is carried out *across* panels; that is, the size of the display is set such that the mean absolute orientation of the line segments making up *all* of the loess curves is a 45 degree angle.

The data in Figure 6.4 tell a fairly straightforward story. Recall that the state partisanship and ideology variables are coded so that larger values indicate more Democratic and liberal electorates, respectively. The smooth curves in the given panels are all approximately linear, with a positive slope that is relatively constant across the panels. This shows that Clinton vote percentage increases as state electorates become more Democratic. Furthermore, the stability in the orientations of the loess curves shows that the nature of this relationship is not affected by state ideology. The *locations* of the curves do vary somewhat, shifting upward from the leftmost to the rightmost panel. This trend can be discerned quite readily by comparing the positions of the loess curves and the grid lines within each panel. Doing so shows that the *level* of Clinton voting increases as state electorates become more liberal. The stability of the three loess curves, however, indicates that the *effect* of partisanship is relatively constant, regardless of state ideology.

For present purposes, the most important information gleaned from the trellis display in Figure 6.4 involves the series of linear loess curves that shift their vertical positions smoothly from one conditioning panel to the next within the respective trellis displays. This kind of pattern shows that electorate partisanship is linearly related to Clinton vote percentages, and that these effects seem to be additive with respect to the influence of electorate ideology. It is important to emphasize that this pattern arose from the data themselves and not as a result of any prior specifications on the part of the researcher. The fact that linear, additive functional relationships appeared when they were not constrained to do so provides very strong evidence that a relatively straightforward multiple regression equation would be perfectly adequate for modeling the structure within these data. Thus, a multivariate graphical display provides useful information for fitting a numeric statistical model.

Plots With Several Conditioning Variables

The conditioning plots presented so far have all contained trivariate data. Each one has shown how a single dependent variable varies as a function of two other variables. The conditioning plot display strategy can be generalized easily to include larger numbers of variables. This is accomplished by specifying more than one conditioning variable. The panels of the display would then show the bivariate relationship between the dependent variable and the panel variable, within each distinct *combination* of sliced intervals from the full set of conditioning variables.

Figure 6.5 shows how the coplot display method would be generalized to incorporate two conditioning variables simultaneously. The graph uses the state-level crime data to display the relationship between law enforcement spending and property crime rates while controlling for per capita income and log population density. To do so, the coplot now contains two separate given panels. The first given panel, shown horizontally in the top margin, indicates that per capita income is sliced into six overlapping intervals; in fact, these are the same conditioning intervals that were used earlier. The second given panel is oriented in a vertical direction, and it is placed in the rightmost column margin of the coplot. This given panel shows that log population density is sliced into four overlapping conditioning intervals (once again, there is approximately 75% overlap between adjacent intervals).

The placement of the two given panels leads to a straightforward interpretation of the differences across the dependence panels. The columns of the display correspond to variability in per capita income, with values increasing from left to right. The rows of the display correspond to variability in log population density, with values increasing from bottom to top. Thus, scanning across any row shows how the relationship between crime rates and law enforcement spending is affected by the level of per capita income, while holding log population density fixed at a specific interval of values. Similarly, scanning up or down within any column reveals how the bivariate relationship is affected by log population density, while holding per capita income constant.

Let us begin by examining the dependence panels in rows 1 through 3 of the display (that is, the three lowest rows). In each one, the loess curve fitted to the data points indicates that the relationship between the dependent variable and the panel variable is sharply positive. Superficially, there may appear to be a few departures from these patterns, such as the "hockey stick" shapes of the curves in panels (6, 1) and (6, 3). Closer inspection, however, reveals that the direction reversals in both of these smooth curves are largely due to a single point in the respective panels. They do not seem to signal any substantively important nonlinearity in the functional relationship between crime rates and law enforcement spending.

Next, consider the dependence panels in row 4—the topmost row of the coplot. Here, the loess curves change their orientations across the columns. Starting at the left side, panel (1, 4) shows the now-familiar sharp positive slope. Then, the curve flattens out gradually as we scan across the panels toward the right, until it is nearly horizontal in panel (6, 4). Note, however, that some caution is necessary when interpreting the information in this row. For one thing, the data points in panel (1, 4) show hardly any variability on the law enforcement spending variable, so the loess curve may not provide a very reliable representation of the functional relationship

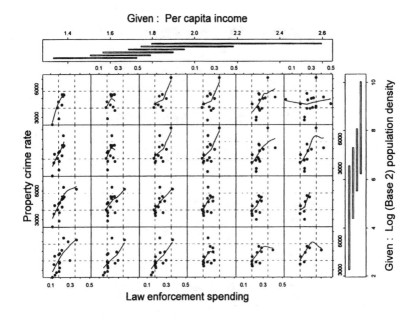

Figure 6.5. Coplot of 1992 State Property Crime Rates Versus Law Enforcement Spending, Conditioning on Per Capita Income and Log Population Density

at this combination of conditioning values. At the same time, there is a discrepant data point that shows up near the top of the data rectangle in several panels, indicating a single state with an unusually high property crime rate given its values on the other variables. This bivariate outlier affects the loess fit in several panels, such as (3, 4), (4, 4), and (5, 4). By doing so, this single data point obscures the change in the orientation of the smooth curve across the panels.

The information in Figure 6.5 indicates that the earlier conclusions reported about these data must be revised somewhat. There now seems to be an interaction effect involving three, rather than two, variables. At moderate to low levels of log population density, the relationship between law enforcement spending and property crime rates is uniformly positive, regardless of per capita income levels. In states with the largest population densities, however, the functional dependence becomes much less pronounced as income increases. At the highest levels of per capita income, densely populated states show no relationship at all between spending on law enforcement and the amount of property crime.

68

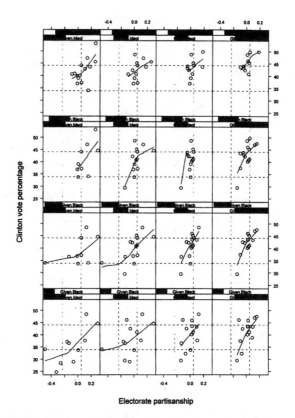

Figure 6.6. Trellis Display of 1992 State Vote Percentage for Clinton Versus Electorate Partisanship, Conditioned on Electorate Ideology and Relative Size of State African American Population

Figure 6.6 shows a trellis display with two conditioning variables, using the 1992 state voting data. Here, Clinton vote percentages are shown as a function of electorate partisanship, controlling for both electorate ideology and the relative size of each state's black population (expressed as a percentage of the total population). Both of the conditioning variables are sliced into four intervals with 75% overlap between adjacent intervals. Just as with the simpler trellis displays discussed earlier, the conditioning intervals are still shown by the strip labels at the top of each dependence panel. Now, though, there are two strips for each panel, showing the simultaneous combination of conditioning values that generated the subset of data points shown in that panel.

Inspection of the shaded rectangles in the panel strips of Figure 6.6 shows that ideology varies within each row; at each level of black population, state electorates become more liberal (i.e., larger values of the ideology variable) moving from left to right across the columns. The conditioning intervals for black population are shown within each column, with the percentage of African Americans increasing from the lowest row to the top. Note also that the distribution of state black populations is strongly skewed toward positive values: This is indicated by the differences in the widths of the four conditioning slices for this variable. Specifically, the three lowest slices are each about the same width (covering about one-fourth of the variable's overall range), and they barely shift their positions from left to right. This corresponds to a very high concentration of observations at this region of the distribution. The fourth conditioning interval is much wider than any of the others, indicating the presence of a long tail in the right side of the distribution.

Substantively, the information in the trellis display shows that the relationship between partisanship and Clinton votes remains even after state ideology and racial composition are taken into account. The loess curves are relatively straight, with very similar orientations in all the dependence panels. Bends in the smooth curves generally can be attributed to outlying observations. At the same time, each panel contains a fairly small number of observations, so variations in the slopes of the curves probably should not be taken too seriously. Thus, the effects of electorate partisanship on state voting outcomes seem to be relatively impervious to influences from other variables.

The examples presented in this section should suffice to illustrate how conditioning plots can be generalized to incorporate a number of separate variables. Here, different conditioning variables are allocated to different dimensions—the rows and columns—of the graphical display. Of course, further adjustments would be necessary if there are more than two conditioning variables. One approach would be to subdivide the row/columns to show two (or more) conditioning variables in a single physical dimension of the display. Another possibility would be to spread the dependence panels across separate pages (or screens), with each page corresponding to a single slice of a conditioning variable.

In principle, conditioning plots could be generalized to incorporate any number of variables by further subdividing the dependence panels; however, there are some practical limitations to this process. Each new conditioning variable increases the number of panels in the display by a factor equal to the number of its conditioning intervals. Therefore, a sizable number of variables will result in a very large graph, which can be quite difficult to comprehend. For this reason, most conditioning plots incorporate only a few variables. This is not a particularly onerous constraint. For one thing, a graphical display containing a small number of variables is fully consistent with the overall statistical objective of parsimonious representations for data. Also, as we already have seen, even relatively simple conditioning plots can generate an enormous amount of interesting information about the data. More complicated displays therefore are frequently unnecessary.

General Principles for Conditioning Plots

There are several guidelines and general principles that are helpful for using the conditioning plot display strategy. First, a conditioning plot usually contains an enormous amount of data and therefore requires careful study to maximize the amount of usable information that can be extracted from it. It is simply too easy to overlook important details in a superficial visual survey of the overall multipanel display. For example, we already have seen several cases where a single outlier has a pronounced effect on the smooth curve fitted in a dependence panel. The source of these apparent nonlinearities would have been missed if we had focused strictly on the curves and ignored the underlying, individual data points that produced them. The lesson is simple to articulate but often difficult to carry out in practice: Give careful scrutiny to all the information contained in a conditioning plot.

Second, it usually is necessary to examine several different conditioning plots for any set of multivariate data. This is particularly true in contexts where a single dependent variable is considered to be a function of several (say, $k - 1$) explanatory variables. In such cases, it is best to create $k - 1$ separate multipanel displays. This gives each independent variable a chance to serve as the panel variable, conditioned on all the others. This is really the only way to obtain a graphical representation of each explanatory variable's *net* impact, after removing any confounding effects from the other variables (Becker et al., 1995; Cleveland, 1994b).

Third, the individual panels of the conditioning plot should be arranged in a way that facilitates visual recognition of patterns within the data. The dependence panels should be located so that the sliced intervals vary in a regular progression, both within rows and across columns. This allows for efficient visual processing of any variability in the relationship between the dependent variable and the panel variable; the analyst simply scans across a single dimension of the display (say, across rows within a column, or vice versa) to observe how the bivariate structure changes with the conditioning slices.

Fourth, it is important to make the information about the conditioning variables as clear as possible. In fact, this is precisely the feature that distinguishes between the three types of conditioning plots presented in this chapter. Casement plots use verbal descriptions of the conditioning information for each dependence panel. Coplots use a separate given panel for each conditioning variable. Trellis displays show the conditioning slices in the strip labels for each dependence panel. Although exactly the same information can be presented in each case, it is progressively easier and more convenient to understand in the respective kinds of conditioning plots.[18]

Fifth, the aspect ratio of the panels in a conditioning plot can be extremely important. Visual perception of smooth curves is optimized by banking them to an absolute orientation of 45 degrees (Cleveland, McGill, & McGill, 1988). With multipanel displays, the aspect ratio should be fixed whenever possible so that the mean absolute orientation of *all* fitted curves, across the various panels, is set to 45 degrees. The reasoning is straightforward: The basic objective of the conditioning plot is to see how a bivariate relationship varies, conditional on other variables. The within-panel structure often is depicted by adding a smooth curve to the data points; then, the analyst determines whether this curve changes across the panels. Visual perception of differences in the curves is most accurate when these differences are maximized, and this, in turn, occurs when the curves are banked to 45 degrees. This process may result in some coplots that have rather strange aspect ratios from an aesthetic perspective; nevertheless, banking to 45 degrees is a very useful tool for drawing out the greatest possible amount of information from the graphical display.

A sixth detail of the conditioning plot display strategy involves the scale lines and labels used in the display. As explained earlier, it is crucial that the scale lines used for the bivariate scatterplots remain constant across the full set of dependence panels. This creates a redundancy in the display, which eliminates the need to include variable, scale, and tick mark labels for every panel. The dependent and panel variables are labeled only in the outside margins of the outermost dependence panels of the conditioning plot. Similarly, tick marks are shown only on the outside edges of the display. Tick labels for the dependent variable are shown alternately, in the left and right exterior margins, while the tick labels for the panel variable are given in alternate top and bottom margins. This strategy provides the analyst with plenty of information to look up approximate data values for specific observations. At the same time, it maximizes the data-ink ratio, and therefore focuses attention more directly on the most important component of the conditioning plot—the data themselves.

Finally, the dependence panels of a conditioning plot usually contain grid lines, even though the latter are specifically *not* recommended for the data rectangle of a bivariate scatterplot. The reason for this is that grid lines facilitate comparisons across panels in the coplot (Cleveland, 1994). They provide a stable visual reference within the interior of the panels, which makes it much easier to discern differences in the relative positions of panel-specific point clouds, the orientations of smooth curves, and so on. Therefore, grid lines serve an important purpose for interpreting the information contained within a conditioning plot. The grids themselves must be relatively unobtrusive; they should not interfere with visual detection of the data points or any other information that is presented within the display.

Conclusions

The discussion in this chapter has shown how conditioning plots can be used to examine relatively complex functional relationships among sets of variables. At this point, it is perhaps useful to place this topic within the broader context of the monograph: Conditional plots provide the analyst with a relatively unadorned view *into* the data space. They do so by breaking the relatively complicated, multidimensional space down into a set of simpler and more readily visualizable components. More specifically, the dependence panels of the conditioning plot show a series of adjacent, and possibly overlapping, "slabs" within the overall k-dimensional space. Then, each of these slabs are "flattened" to form the dependence panels. Finally, the "flattened slabs" are arranged next to each other on a two-dimensional surface, to create the actual conditioning plot display.

Note the relationship between the multidimensional original data space and the layout of the graphical display. For example, assume that a conditioning plot shows the relationship between two variables, X_1 and Y, within sliced intervals of another variable, X_2. As one scans across the separate dependence panels in the conditioning plot, it is equivalent to moving along the X_2 direction in the data space, while maintaining a viewing perspective that is orthogonal to the plane formed by the scale axes for variables X_1 and Y. Thus, the conditioning plot might be conceptualized as a static record of a "tour" along a specified direction through the multidimensional data space.

In conclusion, conditioning plots show multivariate data in a form that is highly organized and readily understandable, through visual inspection. Thus, casement plots, coplots, and trellis displays all achieve the more general objectives of statistical graphics: They enable a researcher to discern patterns within a complex dataset without requiring overly stringent assumptions about the nature and details of any underlying structure that may exist among the data points.

7. THE BIPLOT

The graphical displays considered so far in this monograph all present a somewhat asymmetric view of multivariate data. According to data theory, a datum always consists of a relationship among a pair of distinct objects—usually, an observation and a variable. A typical display will show only one of these kinds of objects. In other words, graphical methods, such as scatterplots, conditioning plots, or icon plots, portray the observations directly, using the plotting symbols themselves. The variables on which the observations are measured receive only an implicit representation, in the axes (in the case of the scatterplot or its variants) or the varying properties of the plotting symbols (in the case of icon plots). This chapter will discuss a different kind of display strategy called the *biplot* (Gabriel 1971, 1981; Gower & Hand, 1996).

The purpose of the biplot is to show variables and observations together, in a way that represents graphically their joint interrelationships. A biplot is usually presented as a two-dimensional display. Note, however, that the "bi-" prefix in the term "biplot" refers to the two kinds of objects included in the graph, and not to the dimensionality of the pictorial representation. In fact, the basic method is easily generalized to create three-dimensional (or even more highly dimensioned) biplots.

Construction of a Biplot

The biplot graphs variables as vectors and observations as points together within a common space. These geometric objects are located in such a way that observation i's value on variable j is modeled by the scalar product between the point representing i and the vector representing j. A scalar product is a numeric value that is obtained by taking the sum of the products of corresponding elements in two vectors. To explain further, assume that X is an n by k data matrix, with $n > k$ (i.e., more observations than variables). The variables are centered, so that their respective means are all zero. If they are measured in different units, the variables are also usually standardized to unit variances. In any event, the data matrix can be factored, as follows:

(7.1)
$$X = A\,B'$$

In this equation, A is an $n \times p$ matrix, which can be interpreted as the coordinates for the n observation points along p rectangular (i.e., orthogonal) axes. Similarly, B is a $k \times p$ matrix, which represents the coordinates for the k variables along the same p axes. Note that the value of p will be discussed below; for now, it is sufficient to note that $p \leq k$. In Equation 7.1, the cells of the product matrix, X, are obtained by taking the scalar product of the appropriate row in A (i.e., a row vector) and the appropriate column in B' (i.e., a column vector), as follows:

(7.2)
$$x_{ij} = \sum_{r=1}^{p} a_{ir}\, b_{rj}'$$

Equation 7.2 shows that one particular data value (i.e., falling at the intersection of the ith row and the jth column of X) is obtained by combining the information for the ith observation (contained in the ith row of A) and the information for the jth variable (contained in the jth column of B').

The numerical entries in the matrices A and B are defined by a singular value decomposition of the data matrix, X. The singular value decomposition is a very important matrix operation, with many applications in statistics and data analysis. More complete discussions can be found in Weller and Romney (1990), any linear algebra text (e.g., Green & Carroll, 1976), and most works on multivariate statistics (e.g., Krzanowski, 1990).

To obtain A and B, the singular value decomposition is employed to factor X into three other matrices, as follows:

(7.3)
$$X = U\,D\,V'$$

In this equation, U is the $n \times p$ matrix of orthogonal left singular vectors, D is the p by p diagonal matrix of singular values, and V is the k by p matrix of orthogonal right singular vectors. Informally, one could think of the singular vectors as different, independent, sources of variability in the data. The value of p therefore is equal to the rank of X. If no variable is defined as a perfect linear combination of the others (i.e., the variables are all linearly independent), then $p = k$.

The singular values (i.e., the diagonal entries in $\mathbf{D}$) indicate how much contribution the respective singular vectors give to the overall sum of squares in $\mathbf{X}$. Each singular value (say, $\mathbf{d}_r$) is associated with a particular pair of singular vectors ($\mathbf{u}_r$ and $\mathbf{v}_r$). They are arrayed along the diagonal cells of $\mathbf{D}$ from largest to smallest.

Next, let $\mathbf{A}_{[2]}$ be the $n \times 2$ matrix of biplot coordinates for the observation points. Also, let $\mathbf{B}_{[2]}$ be the $k \times 2$ matrix of biplot coordinates for the variables. These two matrices are obtained as follows:

(7.4a) $$\mathbf{A}_{[2]} = \mathbf{U}_{[2]}\mathbf{D}_{[2]}{}^{c}$$

(7.4b) $$\mathbf{B}_{[2]} = \mathbf{V}_{[2]}\mathbf{D}_{[2]}{}^{1-c}$$

In these equations, $\mathbf{U}_{[2]}$ and $\mathbf{V}_{[2]}$ are the first two columns of $\mathbf{U}$ and $\mathbf{V}$, respectively, and $\mathbf{D}_{[2]}$ is the diagonal matrix formed by the first two singular values. The value of c in the superscripts on $\mathbf{D}_{[2]}$ can vary between 0 and 1; it represents the degree to which the variability in the data is reflected in the observation points or in the variable points. Typically, c is set to 0.5; this partitions the variance equally to observations and variables. Geometrically, setting c to 0.5 scales the coordinates so that the observations and the variables fall within the same region of the plotting space.[19]

Finally, each row of $\mathbf{A}_{[2]}$ is plotted as a point in a two-axis coordinate system. The rows of $\mathbf{B}_{[2]}$ are also plotted within the same space, but they are shown differently, as the terminal points of directed line segments emanating from the origin. Thus, observations and variables can be easily identified and distinguished from each other through visual inspection of the biplot.[20]

Biplot Approximation of the Data

The scalar product of the two coordinate matrices produces an $n \times k$ matrix, as follows:

(7.5) $$\mathbf{X}_{[2]} = \mathbf{A}_{[2]}\mathbf{B}_{[2]}'$$

Note that whenever $k > 2$, then $\mathbf{X}_{[2]}$ is only an approximation of the original data matrix rather than an exact representation. Of course, this occurs because the biplot employs only the first two columns from the singular value decomposition; therefore, the biplot really does not contain all of the information from the data. The correspondence between $X_{[2]}$ and X nevertheless often is quite close.

The singular value decomposition is a variance-maximizing transformation of X. This means that the first q singular vectors and values are the q-factor linear combinations that will most accurately reproduce the original variance contained in X. The points and vectors in the biplot therefore represent the *best* possible two-dimensional approximation of the original data. In this context, the term "best" should be interpreted in the least-squares sense; in other words, the entries in $A_{[2]}B_{[2]}'$ exhibit the maximum possible correlation with the corresponding cells of X (Eckart & Young, 1936; Greenacre, 1984). Accordingly, the biplot should capture as much of the original information as is possible within a two-dimensional summary of the original, k-dimensional data space.

The adequacy of the biplot approximation to the data matrix is measured by the degree to which the first two columns of the singular value decomposition account for the variance in the original data. Specifically, the sum of all p squared singular values equals the total sum of squares in the data matrix:

(7.6)
$$\sum_{r=1}^{p} d_r^2 = \sum_{j=1}^{k} \sum_{i=1}^{n} (x_{ij} - \overline{X}_j)^2$$

The square of each singular value, say d_r^2, measures the contribution of the corresponding pair of singular vectors to the total sum of squares in the data—in this case, the rth column of U and the rth row of V'. This leads to the following goodness of fit measure for a two-dimensional biplot:

(7.7)
$$R^2 = \frac{d_1^2 + d_2^2}{\sum_{r=1}^{p} d_r^2}$$

The expression on the right-hand side of Equation 7.7 measures the sum of the first two singular values as a proportion of the total sum of squared singular values; therefore, it can be interpreted in a manner similar to the variance in the data that is included in the graphical model provided by the biplot.

Interpreting the Contents of the Biplot

The great advantage of a biplot is that its components can be interpreted very easily. First, correlations among the variables are related to the angles between the vectors, or more specifically, to the cosines of these angles. An acute angle (i.e., one less than 90 degrees) between two vectors indicates a positive correlation between the two corresponding variables, while obtuse angles (greater than 90 degrees) indicate negative correlation. Angles of 0 or 180 degrees indicate perfect positive or negative correlation, respectively. A pair of orthogonal vectors (separated by a 90 degree, right angle) represents a correlation of zero.

Next, consider the observations, which are represented by points in the biplot. The distances between the points correspond to the similarities between the observation profiles. Recall that the profile for observation i is defined as i's array of scores on all k variables. Two observations with scores that are relatively similar across all the variables will be depicted as points that fall relatively close to each other within the two-dimensional space used for the biplot. Conversely, observations that differ a great deal from each other will be shown as points at widely separated locations within the space.

The value or score for any observation (say, i) on any variable (say, X_j) is related to the perpendicular projection from the point for i to the line that is collinear with the vector for X_j. If the score x_{ij} is a positive value, then the projection will fall on the X vector itself. If x_{ij} is a negative value, then the projection will fall on the line corresponding to X, but in the direction that is exactly opposite to that of the X vector. The farther away from the origin that an observation's perpendicular projection falls, the more extreme that observation's value on that variable (in either the positive or negative direction). This property ensures that the vectors will be oriented so they point toward the observations that have the largest values on their respective variables.

Example of a Biplot

Figure 7.1 shows a biplot of some data on 1992 policy expenditures in the American states. The data matrix that produced this graph contains 48 rows (each representing one state) and six columns (each representing one

78

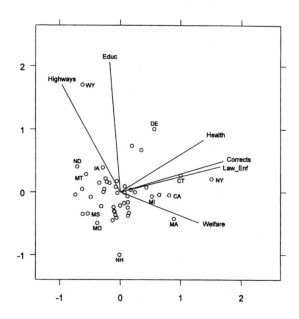

Figure 7.1. Biplot of 1992 State Policy Spending*

*Biplot is constructed from a symmetric factorization of the data matrix.

policy area). As recommended earlier, the variables were standardized to zero means and unit variances before carrying out the singular value decomposition. Doing so has several advantages. For one thing, the unit variances remove differences in measurement units that could also lead to differential effects on the singular value decomposition of the data. This is not really a problem with these data, because the original measurement units are the same for all the variables—thousands of dollars per capita. On the other hand, centering the variables removes the different mean values and eliminates "level effects" that may otherwise exist across the different variables. If states routinely spent more on one policy area relative to the others, then that one column of the data matrix would have a stronger impact on the results of the factorization (and vice versa, for smaller data values). This is a problem with the original data values used here; as explained in Chapter 3, states almost always spend more on education than any of the other policies, and they all tend to spend relatively small amounts on corrections.

Standardizing the variables also produces some geometric properties that are helpful for interpreting the information in the biplot. The origin of the space corresponds to the location of the means on all the variables in the display. An observation's distance from the origin (regardless of direction) therefore summarizes the extremity of the scores in that observation's profile of variable values. Similarly, the unit variances affect the vector lengths: The squared length of a variable's vector corresponds to the proportion of that variable's variance that is represented in the two-dimensional coordinate space contained in the biplot. If a variable's variance were fully represented in the biplot, then the length of its vector would be 1.0; alternatively, if the biplot only represented half of a variable's total variance, then the length of its vector would be 0.71 (or $\sqrt{.50}$), and so on.

First, consider the goodness of fit for the biplot. There are six singular values (the rank of the data matrix is 6, because the variables are linearly independent). The sum of the squared singular values is equal to 282; the latter value is, itself, equal to the total sum of squares in the standardized data matrix. The first two singular values (i.e., the ones used to form the two coordinate axes in the biplot) are 10.159 and 8.522. These values are substituted into Equation 7.7 to obtain the R^2 value:

$$R^2 = \frac{10.159^2 + 8.522^2}{282} = \frac{103.20 + 72.62}{282} = 0.624$$

Thus, the biplot in Figure 7.1 represents about 62% of the total variance in the standardized spending data.

A great deal of information can be drawn from the biplot in Figure 7.1. First, consider the variables. The vector orientations show that the policy areas are divided into two relatively distinct clusters. One of the clusters is composed of highway and education spending; the other combines expenditures on health care, welfare, law enforcement, and corrections. State expenditures are positively correlated for policies that fall within the respective clusters; this is indicated by the small angles between policy vectors within the two clusters. The most pronounced example of this involves spending on law enforcement and on corrections. The vectors for these two policy areas are nearly collinear with each other. Accordingly, the cosine and, hence, the correlation between the values on the two variables also is quite large.

In contrast, expenditures are either negatively correlated or virtually uncorrelated *across* the two clusters of policies. The clearest illustration of this pattern involves highways and welfare. The vectors for these two policy areas point in nearly opposite directions; therefore, states that spend large amounts of money to build and maintain roads generally spend less money providing for their needy citizens, and vice versa. Welfare spending also is negatively correlated with education spending, but the pattern is much weaker; this is shown by the smaller angular separation between the welfare vector and the education vector. Still, the angle between these vectors is larger than 90 degrees, so states that allocate money toward one of these policy areas are less likely to allocate money toward the other.

One more interesting feature of the variables shown in the biplot is the nearly perpendicular orientation of the vectors for highway and for health care. The angle between these vectors is approximately 90 degrees, so the cosine is very close to zero. This, in turn, shows that the values on these two variables are uncorrelated. The amount of money that a state spends on highways is simply unrelated to the money that it devotes to health care, and vice versa.

Next, let us consider the states. Notice that some of the points in Figure 7.1 have been labeled with two-letter abbreviations. Most of these labels are near the periphery of the point cloud. This avoids the excessive overplotting that would result if all the state points were given labels, and it still enables the identification of several interesting features within the dataset.

The direction from lower left to upper right in the display (roughly parallel to the vector for health care) corresponds to the overall level of state spending, without regard to particular policy areas. States like Mississippi, Missouri, and New Hampshire all have low per capita expenditure values. Their points are located in the region of the space opposite to the directions in which the spending vectors are pointed; this shows that their data values fall below the mean on most of the variables. In contrast, states like New York and Delaware are located closest to the "northeast" region of the biplot, and these are precisely the two states that spend large amounts per capita, across the board, on all the policy areas.

There are also some substantive spending patterns that are readily discernible in Figure 7.1. For example, notice that the points in the rightmost area of the display correspond to heavily populated, urban states, such as New York, Connecticut, California, and Massachusetts. Perpendicular projections from these points would fall at fairly extreme, positive locations along the variable vectors for welfare, law enforcement, corrections, and health care. This seems very reasonable, given the human service demands and public order problems often experienced in these states. At the other extreme, most of the points in the upper left region of the biplot represent western states, including North Dakota, Montana, Iowa, and Wyoming. These points have large, positive perpendicular projections onto the vector representing highways, and negative perpendicular projections on the welfare vector. Given their large geographic areas, potentially extreme weather conditions, and low population densities, the corresponding spending patterns for these states (i.e., a lot on highway construction/maintenance and not as much on human services) make a great deal of sense.

Variations of the Basic Biplot

Figure 7.1 shows the most commonly used type of biplot. There are many variations, however, of this basic display. One possibility would be to alter the value of c in the exponent on the D matrix, back in Equations 7.4a and 7.4b. Doing so results in different partitions of the variance in the data. For example, setting $c = 1$ results in the following, which is sometimes called the JK' factorization of the data:

(7.8a) $$A = U D$$

(7.8b) $$B = V'$$

Figure 7.2A shows a biplot constructed using Equations 7.8a and 7.8b for the standardized state spending data. This version of the biplot focuses most directly on the observations. In other words, allocating all the variance in the singular values to the A matrix guarantees that the distances between the points in the biplot will be the closest possible two-dimensional approximation to the summed differences between the row profiles in the data matrix.

Still another factorization, sometimes called the GH' version, allocates the singular values to the columns of the data matrix, as follows:

(7.9a) $$A = U$$

(7.9b) $$B = D V'$$

82

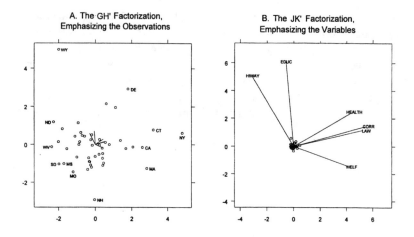

Figure 7.2. Biplots Created From Different Factorizations of the Data Matrix

The resultant biplot is shown in Figure 7.2B. In this case, the graph represents the structure in the variables most directly, in the sense that the cosines of the angles between the vectors are the best possible two-dimensional approximations to the correlations between the variables.

The two biplots shown in Figure 7.2 are both affected by an obvious problem: The pictorial representation of one object set from the data matrix (i.e., either observations or variables) is very large, relative to that of the other object set. In Figure 7.2A, the graphical display focuses on the observations. Therefore, the point cloud takes up most of the plotting region while the vectors are "squeezed in" close to the origin of the space. The opposite is true in Figure 7.2B, where the variable vectors are very large, while the cloud of observation points forms a largely indistinguishable mass in the center.

The kinds of biplots shown in Figure 7.2 might be helpful when the researcher is particularly interested in either the observations or the variables; however, they are seldom used in practice. The problem is that the differences in scale that occur across the vectors and the points inhibit visual perception of the "smaller" object set within the graphical display. In addition, there is really very little advantage gained by using one of the asymmetric factorizations: The cosines and the interpoint distances in

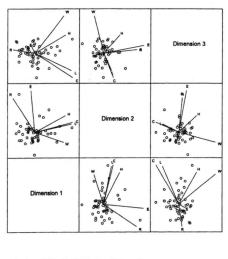

Key to variable abbreviations: C Corrections
                                E Education
                                H Health care
                                L Law enforcement
                                R Highways
                                W Welfare

Figure 7.3. Three-Dimensional Biplot Matrix of 1992 State Policy Spending
Data*

NOTE: C = corrections, E = education, H = health care, L = law enforcement, R = highways, and
W = welfare.
*Biplots are constructed from a three-dimensional, symmetric factorization of the data matrix.

either the *GH'* or *JK'* versions will still only be approximations of the actual
data values whenever the number of variables (or more generally, the
smaller dimension of **X**) is larger than three.

Accordingly, it seems reasonable to employ the symmetric factorization,
as shown back in Equations 7.4a and 7.4b. The angular separations in the
resultant biplot are still inversely related to the values of the correlations,
and the interpoint distances will still be directly related to overall differences in data values across observations. Because the points and vectors
will tend to fill the same region of the space, however, it should be much
easier to discern structure and details involving both the observations and
variables from the data matrix.

Another variation would be to generalize the "flat" two-dimensional biplot
into multiple dimensions. The reason for doing so would be to obtain a
graph that represents a larger portion of the variance in the original data

matrix. A three-dimensional biplot is obtained by taking the first three singular vectors and values from **X**, a four-dimensional biplot would use the first four, and so on.

Thus, the procedure for constructing a multidimensional biplot is a straightforward generalization of the methods used in the two-dimensional case. The difficulties arise in the graphical presentation. One possibility is to construct a "biplot matrix" similar to the scatterplot matrix, as discussed in Chapter 5. In this case, the plotting cells of the matrix would be defined by the scaled singular vectors and the overall display would show all possible combinations of two-dimensional biplots for a given dataset.[21]

A three-dimensional biplot matrix for the state spending data is shown in Figure 7.3. This display represents approximately 76% of the total variance in the data matrix. The R^2 is obtained by summing the squares of the first three singular vectors and expressing the sum as a proportion of the total sum of squares in **X**. This value is about a 14% improvement over the fit of the two-dimensional biplot. The variance-maximizing nature of the singular value decomposition ensures that each additional dimension will account for the maximum possible amount of additional variance in the data.

Note that the individual cells in Figure 7.3 contain very little adornment. Just like the scatterplot matrix, most of the details are omitted to facilitate visual scanning across adjacent cells. For this reason, the observation points are not labeled, and simple, one-letter labels are used for the variable vectors, with explanations given in the graph legend.

Figure 7.3 is based on a symmetric factorization of the data; therefore, the contents of cell (2, 1) are identical to the original two-dimensional biplot from Figure 7.1, and cell (1, 2) shows a transposed version of the same biplot. The "new" information is shown in the top row and the rightmost column of the matrix, where the cells all involve the third singular vector. These views of the data break up one of the original clusters of variables identified earlier.

The third singular vector serves primarily to distinguish corrections and law enforcement spending from welfare. The vectors for these variables were all separated by relatively small angles in the two-dimensional representation, but the vector for welfare and those for law enforcement and corrections point in opposite directions along the third coordinate axis. In this manner, the three-dimensional biplot generates a graphical representation that provides a closer depiction of the correlational structure underlying the variables in the original data matrix.

Conclusions

The biplot reveals a great deal of information about the structure contained in a multivariate dataset. This graphical display is useful for such tasks as summarizing intercorrelations among the variables, isolating clusters of observations, and identifying unusual observations. It is important to emphasize that such insights are gained from the graphical evidence alone, because the specific values along a biplot's coordinate axes are not usually interpretable in any substantive terms.

It also is important, however, to recognize that the biplot display strategy does have some weaknesses. Even though a biplot contains graphical objects for all the variables and the observations, it still presents a rather incomplete picture of the underlying information. The biplot's effectiveness depends on the extent to which the variability in the dataset can be captured by linear relationships within a low-dimensional space. If some of the variables behave in an idiosyncratic manner (compared to the others) or if the variables conform to nonlinear structures, then a biplot will result in a distorted view of the information within the data matrix.

Because of the preceding limitations, critics could charge that the biplot fails to achieve two of the most important advantages usually associated with a graphical approach to data analysis: (a) The biplot does not show all the data, and (b) it is based on an a priori assumption about the structure underlying the data (linearity). These problems can be addressed through careful preliminary work, including the selection of appropriate sets of variables, and inspection of the component bivariate relationships (probably using a scatterplot matrix) to identify any troublesome nonlinearities. After any such problems are diagnosed and remedied, the biplot can serve as a very concise display strategy—one that is capable of incorporating a great deal of information within a single, easily interpretable graphical summary.

8. CONCLUSIONS

This monograph has presented a number of tools for visualizing multivariate data. Although the successive chapters have treated the different graphical displays as separate techniques, it is important to emphasize that there is actually a great deal of continuity among them. Most generally, all the methods discussed above provide strategies for taking the information contained within multidimensional arrays and representing it as a series of two-dimensional sets of values. Geometrically, this corresponds to a *k*-dimensional space (usually composed of observation-points within variable axes) whose information is projected onto a two-dimensional surface. The latter is advantageous, of course, because two-dimensional information can be displayed readily in pictorial form.

It is really only the details involved in making the transition from multiple dimensions into two dimensions that change from one type of display to the next. Some graphical displays actually "look into" the data space itself. These include three-dimensional scatterplots, bubble plots, scatterplot matrices, and conditioning plots. Such methods are helpful because observers can rely on everyday notions of physical space to interpret differences among the objects within the data.

Other display procedures make no attempt to provide a physical model of the data space. Instead, glyph plots, profile plots, and related methods depict variability among observations in a completely symbolic manner. Doing so may strike some readers as a bit unusual, but it is important to emphasize that physical analogies are inherently limiting. Multiple-code plotting icons therefore can be an effective means of overcoming the "curse of dimensionality" that is encountered with multivariate data.

Still another set of display methods employs mathematical summarizations of the information in the data matrix. The biplot uses two separate, but related, linear transformations of the data matrix to show observations and variables within a common viewing perspective. Even though the latter does not provide a direct view of the original data space, the geometric construction is such that most of the interesting information can be observed in simple geometric relationships like angles among vectors and distances between points.

It also is important to emphasize that there are many other display methods that could not be included in the present monograph because of space limitations. For example, *parallel coordinate plots* (e.g., Inselberg, 1985; Wegman, 1990) show observation coordinates along variable axes; however, the axes are lined up next to each other, rather than placed at right angles. Accordingly, each observation is depicted as a series of line segments, which connect that observation's values on the successive, parallel axes. Another possible display is the *Andrews function plot*, which shows each observation as a smooth, cyclical curve within a two-dimensional plotting space (Andrews, 1972). The horizontal axis in this display is an artificial variable, *t*, which varies continuously over some specified interval (usually, $-\pi$ to π). For each observation, the variable plotted on the vertical axis is a k-element function of t, weighted by that observation's values on each of the k variables in the dataset.

Parallel coordinate plots and Andrews function plots are interpreted in somewhat similar ways, even though their physical appearances are quite different. In each case, the analyst examines differences among the shapes and vertical positions of the plotted geometric objects (connected line segments for parallel coordinate plots and smooth curves in Andrews function plots) to discern the amount and nature of the variability among the observations. These display methods are relatively unusual; however, they can be quite useful for showing how observations vary simultaneously across a fairly large number of variables.

Another set of graphs, which Friendly (1991) calls *rectangular displays*, are useful for data that are composed of discrete values and arranged into contingency tables. Basically, these methods show the contents of contingency table cells as a regular array of variably sized rectangles. The exact shapes and positions of the rectangles within the display provide information about the relative sizes of the cell frequencies (Bertin, 1983; Friendly, 1994; Hartigan & Kleiner, 1981). In most cases, rectangular displays convey the amount of deviation that exists between the observed cell frequencies and those that would be expected under a null hypothesis of statistical independence among the variables. Rectangular displays thus provide a pictorial representation of the association between two or more discrete variables.

Finally, this monograph has not considered *active display methods*. These constitute a different strategic approach to graphical data representations, rather than different types of displays per se. Active display methods rely on movement and real-time interactions between the analyst and the data (e.g., Becker, Cleveland, & Wilks, 1988; Young et al., 1993). In contrast, the passive display methods considered in this monograph provide only a stationary representation of the data. The objective, of course, is to find the single "best" view—the one that maximizes the information that can be drawn from the data. The main limitation of passive methods is that it is seldom possible to construct a single graphical display that shows *everything* of interest within a multivariate dataset.

Active graphical methods address the latter problem by changing the content of the graph while the display is under immediate observation. The analyst directly manipulates the viewing perspective on the data space and, in so doing, "looks into" more of the multivariate data than would be discernible in any single, static display. Furthermore, the nature of the changes that occur in the graphical display while "moving" through the data can also provide additional insights about underlying structures and interesting patterns.

Three major techniques are employed in active graphical analyses: Linking, brushing, and spinning. Briefly, *linking* means that several different displays of the same dataset are shown on a computer screen at one time (e.g., two scatterplots, one scatterplot and a histogram, and so on). The displays are connected to each other in the sense that changes made to one display will be reflected in changes that occur simultaneously in the other, linked, displays (Stuetzle, 1987; Young, Faldowski, & Harris, 1990). Linking is very useful for discerning how differences on one variable correspond to variability on other variables.

Brushing is a method for making changes directly to a graphical display. Essentially, a computer pointing device is used to move a "window" (or brush) across the plotting area; when the brush encounters a data point, something about the display changes (Becker & Cleveland, 1987; Becker, Cleveland, & Weil, 1988). For example, the color or shape of the point's plotting symbol may change, an observation label can be displayed, or the observation point could be highlighted both in the display that is being brushed and also in any linked displays that are currently visible on the computer screen. This enables the analyst to focus on a subset of observations and observe its behavior across a number of variables, simultaneously.

Spinning is real-time movement in the viewing perspective on a three-dimensional scatterplot (Becker, Cleveland, & Weil, 1988; Cook & Weisberg, 1994; Huber, 1987). This is a very useful technique that essentially overcomes most of the limitations of the latter display method (as discussed in Chapter 4). Mathematically, the spinning is accomplished through a rotation of the scatterplot; a series of small rotations are successively and quickly applied to the displayed geometric elements (i.e., points and axes). The resultant visual impression is smooth movement of the visible space itself. The ability to "move" the three-dimensional scale cube, relative to the viewing position, provides very useful cues about depth within the display and thereby enhances its importance as an analytic tool.

It is important to emphasize that active graphical methods are very new; they have become feasible research tools only since the development and widespread dissemination of high-resolution, fast displays in desktop computers. There is a great deal of work that is currently being carried out in the subfield of dynamic, interactive graphical methods. For example, there are a variety of methods and strategies for "moving" through k-dimensional space when $k > 3$ (Hurley & Buja, 1990; Young et al., 1988). Such high-dimensional rotations allow the analyst to view a smoothly changing three-dimensional subspace of the full data space. Each three-dimensional view is, itself, a linear combination of the k variables, so relatively standard mathematical rotations can be employed to construct the dynamic views (Young & Rheingans, 1991). The techniques do vary in the strategies that they employ to guide their movements through the space: The *grand tour* moves randomly (Asimov, 1985), the *guided tour* proceeds under the direction of the analyst (Young & Rheingans, 1991), and *projection pursuit* methodology (Friedman, 1987; Huber, 1985) tries to move toward the single most informative direction within the k-dimensional space.

Dynamic, interactive methods are also proving to be useful for working with statistical models; in other words, they provide pictorial representations of structures that are fit to data, rather than the original observations and variables, themselves. Certain analytic methods always have been oriented toward graphical depictions, including factor analysis, multidimensional scaling, and correspondence analysis. Informative graphical representations are also available for many other standard statistical tools, including regression analysis, ANOVA, and MANOVA. Recently, Young and his colleagues developed a general approach called *interactive graphical modeling* that may very well prove useful for all these contexts (Young et al., 1993). In other words, the analyst interacts with the data through a graphical display that represents a statistical structure that has been fitted to the data. To take a very simple example, consider a bivariate scatterplot that shows a regression line fitted to the data points. Assume that the display is shown on a computer screen. The researcher might use a pointing device to move the regression line, relative to the points, to examine the effect on the parameter estimates and the residuals. Or, individual observations might be selectively eliminated from the plot with the placement of the regression line changing to reflect the "new" data to which it is fitted. Both of these simple examples involve "statistical model re-visualization"; in each case, the numerical components of the statistical model would be updated to reflect the changes that are made to the graphical representation. This strategy appears to be very useful for investigating alternative model specifications, checking the influence of outlying observations, and so on. In summary, there are many interesting and exciting techniques that are currently under development in the field of dynamic, interactive statistical graphics.

Of course, there are some drawbacks with active displays. For one thing, there are few, if any, general guidelines for interacting with a multivariate display. At the same time, active methods can become relatively difficult to comprehend when applied to large, complex multivariate datasets.

Perhaps most obvious, it is very difficult to convey the details of an active display in a passive medium, like the pages of a book. For these reasons, static methods, like those considered in most of this monograph, should continue to dominate social scientific applications of statistical graphics for some time in the future.

In conclusion, statistical graphics provide several important advantages for investigating multivariate data. First, well-constructed graphs provide useful, easily comprehensible summaries for large, complicated datasets. Second, graphical summaries of data are relatively resistant to the stringent assumptions that provide the foundations for more traditional, numeric statistical methods. Third, graphical analysis facilitates greater interaction between the researcher and the data. Effective graphical displays for multivariate data show information in ways that reveal patterned regularities, without imposing a priori structure on the empirical observations. This, in turn, facilitates a more comprehensive understanding of the substantive phenomena under investigation.

APPENDIX:
SOFTWARE CONSIDERATIONS

As mentioned at several points in this monograph and in the companion volume (Jacoby, 1997), it is effectively impossible to construct graphical displays for quantitative data using pencil and paper, alone. Part of the problem lies in the computationally intensive nature of many graphical techniques, but it is also a very difficult and time-consuming job to create even a simple graph, containing a relatively moderate number of data points. It is almost impossible to achieve the necessary degree of accuracy in visual representations of numerical information when graphs are drawn by hand. These problems are exacerbated by the fact that graphical data analysis is an interactive process. That is, the first attempt at a graph will usually need to be modified—often several times—before a suitable display is achieved.

For all the preceding reasons, data visualization techniques require the use of a computer with high-resolution graphics capabilities. Given this requirement, most potential users (at least non-programmers) will find themselves constrained by the options that are included in the available software. Written and on-line documentation often can be intimidating, confusing, and incomplete; therefore, this appendix lists the graphical procedures that are contained within a variety of well-known and widely used statistical software packages.

The basic information is presented in Table A.1.[22] The rows of the table correspond to the techniques that are discussed in this monograph and in *Statistical Graphics for Visualizing Univariate and Bivariate Data* (Jacoby,

1997). The columns represent different software platforms. Some of these are stand-alone, full-featured statistical packages (Data Desk, SPSS, Stata, Statgraphics-Plus, Statistica, and SYSTAT). Others represent several variants or components of the same product. For example, S-Plus has its own high-level graphics routines and also includes the separate (but related) Trellis Graphics System; therefore, these are listed as separate software options in Table A.1. Similarly, there are a number of choices for SAS users. For example, the SAS/GRAPH system is an extremely powerful, but somewhat difficult, graphing language. Michael Friendly's (1991) book, *SAS System for Statistical Graphics*, contains a number of macros that create data visualization displays very easily; therefore, these are listed in the column headed "SAS (Friendly)." The SAS system also contains another interactive data analysis component, SAS/IN-SIGHT, which includes a variety of graphical tools (dynamic and interactive displays, as well as passive graphs); therefore, it is listed in a separate column of the table. There is still another SAS product, JMP, which is a smaller, commercial data analysis package with many graphical routines. Finally, ViSta does not really fit into any of the preceding categories. It is described by its creator as an "integrated data analysis environment (Young, 1997)." ViSta is strongly oriented toward data visualization (in fact, "ViSta" stands for "Visual Statistics") and interactive graphical analysis methods. Even though ViSta is not really a full-fledged statistical package, it is a powerful, easy-to-use, and highly flexible computing platform. Addresses and contact information for all these software choices are contained in Table A.2.[23]

It is important to point out that the regular layout of options in Table A.1 belies some of the extreme variety and variability in the software options that are available. For one thing, the terminology is not completely standardized. Some packages therefore say they include "lowess" smoothing, while others employ the term "loess." More seriously, the term "dot plot" is often used to refer to the method that has been identified as a "unidimensional scatterplot" in the present discussion. The term "casement plot" is not actually employed in any of the software documentation. Instead, some of the manuals simply show how multiple displays can be created for subsets of the data, and laid out in a regular grid on the display surface (e.g., Stata and SYSTAT); others call them *categorized graphs* or *3-D spectral plots* (Statistica). Of course, the important thing is the display, rather than the words that are used to identify it; still, the variations in terminology across software packages can be very confusing.

Users also will quickly discover that a certain amount of flexibility, adaptability, and creativity is helpful (and in fact, almost necessary) while conducting a graphical data analysis. For example, many packages do not have an explicit function for jittering data points in a display; however, it is always very easy to simply add a small amount of random variability to the original data and thereby produce jittered values for plotting. As another example, SYSTAT does not have an explicit routine for creating dot plots, but this kind of graph can be produced

Table A.1

Graphical Procedures Available in Software Packages

	Data Desk	JMP	SAS/ INSIGHT	SAS (Friendly)	S-Plus High-Level Graphics	S-Plus Trellis Graphics	SPSS	Stata	Stat-graphics Plus	Statistica	SYSTAT	ViSta
Univariate Graphs												
Basic histogram	X	X	X	X	X	X	X	X	X	X	X	X
Smoothed histogram		X	X	X	X	X		X			X	X
Unidimensional scatterplot	X				X	X		X	X			
Jittering points				X	X	X		X	X		X	
Box plots	X	X	X	X	X	X	X	X	X	X	X	X
Quantile plot		X	X	X	X	X		X		X	X	X
Dot plot				X	X	X		X			X	
Bivariate Graphs												
Basic scatterplot	X	X	X	X	X	X	X	X	X	X	X	X
Rescalable axes	X	X	X	X	X	X	X	X	X	X	X	X
Univariate marginal displays	X		X	X				X		X	X	
Slicing the scatterplot	X		X		X	X						X
Loess smoothing	X			X	X	X	X	X	X		X	
Banking to aspect ratio			X			X					X	
Multivariate Graphs												
Multiple symbols for categorical info	X		X	X	X	X	X	X	X	X	X	X
Glyph symbols in scatterplot				X							X	
Histogram icons					X					X	X	
Polygon icons					X					X	X	
Star icons				X	X	X		X	X	X	X	
Three-dimensional scatterplot	X	X	X	X	X	X	X		X	X	X	X

3-D smoothing, parametric	X					X		X	X
3-D smoothing, nonparametric						X		X	X
Enhancements for 3-D plots	X	X		X		X	X	X	X
3-D real-time rotation	X	X			X	X	X	X	X
Bubble plot			X		X	X		X	X
Scatterplot matrix (SPM)	X	X	X	X	X	X	X	X	X
Half-matrix version of SPM	X			X	X	X		X	X
Univariate info within SPM	X				X	X	X		
Smoothing within SPM panels				X		X		X	X
Casement plot		X		X				X	X
Coplot display			X	X					
Trellis display			X						
Overlapping conditioning slices			X			X			
Biplot display	X	X	X					X	X
Linked plot windows	X	X	X			X	X	X	X
Plot brushing	X	X	X			X	X	X	X
High-dimensional rotation				X					
Parallel coordinate plots	X	X						X	X
Andrews function plots	X	X						X	X
Graphs for Categorical Data									
Rectangular displays	X	X	X						

NOTE: The information in this table is based on programs that were made available to the author during 1996 and early 1997. Most of the packages have been updated since that time, so graphical analysis features may be somewhat different from those listed here.

Table A.2
Addresses and Contact Information for Software Vendors

Address and Telephone	World Wide Web Address
Data Desk Data Description, Inc. 803-573-5121	www.datadesk.com/datadesk/
JMP, SAS/INSIGHT, and SAS/GRAPH SAS Institute Inc. SAS Campus Drive Cary, NC 27513	www.sas.com
S-Plus Statistical Sciences Incorporated, A Division of MathSoft 1700 Westlake Ave. N. Seattle, WA 98109	www.mathsoft.com/splus.html
SPSS and SYSTAT SPSS, Inc. 444 North Michigan Avenue Chicago, IL 60611-3962	www.spss.com
Stata Stata Corporation 702 University Drive East College Station, TX 77840	www.stata.com
STATGRAPHICS Plus Magnugistics, Inc. 2115 East Jefferson Street Rockville, MD 20852-4999	www.statgraphics.com
Statistica StatSoft, Inc. 2325 East 13th Street Tulsa, OK 74104	www.statsoft.com
ViSta Forrest W. Young, L. L. Thurstone Psychometrics Laboratory University of North Carolina Chapel Hill, NC 27599-3270	Software and documentation can be downloaded from the World Wide Web at www.forrest.psych.unc.edu/research/ViSta.html

using the *category plot* that is available in that package. Next, consider the challenges involved in creating a biplot. Apparently, S-Plus and ViSta are the only packages that have routines explicitly designed to generate this kind of display. With most other software, it will be necessary to first perform a principal components analysis to obtain the point and vector coordinates, then overlay two sets of plotting symbols (i.e., vectors and points) within a single scatterplot. It is the author's personal experience that these and similar kinds of problems usually can be handled fairly easily, by exercising some ingenuity. Potential users must be aware of this at the outset and should not be discouraged if their initial results do not produce exactly the kinds of graphical displays desired. Indeed, constructing data graphics actually can be quite fun, and it instills a distinct sense of accomplishment once a complicated graph has been completed successfully.

Even a brief perusal of Table A.1 reveals that most of the commonly used statistical packages contain at least the basic kinds of displays that are useful for univariate, bivariate, and multivariate data. The differences between them tend to lie in the presentational details; for example, default plotting symbols in scatterplots, box widths and whisker styles in box plots, the orientation of the main diagonal in a scatterplot matrix, colors, fill patterns, and so on. Of course, all these kinds of things are secondary concerns compared to the more general objectives of the graphical display itself—showing the data in ways that provide useful insights about the structure and features contained therein. Many (if not most) researchers therefore will find that their usual statistical software package is also perfectly acceptable for graphical purposes.[24]

Nevertheless, the exact nature, capabilities and flexibility of the graphical procedures do vary markedly from one program to the next. Some software packages have special strengths in particular areas. For example, ViSta, Data Desk, SAS/INSIGHT, and JMP are all excellent for interactive analyses with multiple, linked plot windows. ViSta is also undoubtedly the most complete operationalization of an interactive graphical modeling approach to data analysis, including graphical representations of statistical techniques, such as multiple regression, principal components, analysis of variance, and multi-dimensional scaling. S-Plus is clearly the "software of choice" for a variety of procedures, including coplots, trellis displays (particularly with overlapping slices for conditioning variables), loess smoothing (for both bivariate and multivariate data), and banking to a user-specified aspect ratio. At the same time, users may simply like the plotting features and details that exist only in certain programs. For example, both Stata and SYSTAT make it particularly easy to generate many different kinds of sophisticated graphical displays, and Statistica has many options that can be used to produce beautifully rendered, full-color three-dimensional displays.

For all these reasons, many analysts find it helpful to have access to several software packages with graphical capabilities. This, of course, leads to questions about compatibility of data formats. Any such problems usually can be handled very easily. For one thing, software packages are becoming increasingly flexible about reading data that have been stored in different formats. In addition, there are at least two conversion programs that are explicitly designed to move datasets easily across different formats: Stat/Transfer and DBMS/COPY.

There is one other software possibility that should be mentioned: For anyone with even a minimal amount of programming experience, it is a fairly straight-forward task to write special-purpose graphics routines in a programming language or in the programming environments that are now included within several statistical software packages (Stine & Fox, 1996). Examples of the former include LISP-STAT (Tierney, 1990) and APL2STAT (e.g., Fox & Friendly, 1996). Examples of the latter include PROC IML (for *I*nteractive *M*atrix Language) in SAS, ADO files in STATA, the MATRIX routine in SPSS for Windows, and the entire S-PLUS package (particularly the panel functions that are used within the Trellis Graphics System). Various analysts already have made a great deal of progress along these lines, and their results are usually made readily available to interested users in the research community. Useful source material can be found in Stine and Fox (1996) and also within the Michael Friendly's extensive list of statistics and statistical graphics resources, located at the address www.math.yorku.ca/SCS/StatResource.html on the World Wide Web.

It is important to emphasize that software discussions on any subject tend to become outdated very quickly. This is particularly true with a field like data visualization, because graphical presentations of quantitative data currently represent a major area of development in the statistical sciences. The brief discussion presented in this section nevertheless clearly demonstrates that useful software already is widely available. One can only expect that the graphical capabilities of currently existing packages will continue to evolve, becoming more flexible and powerful in the future. Of course, it is certain that new tools will be developed on a regular basis.

NOTES

1. It is also possible to create a geometric representation of the data in which variable points (or more commonly, vectors) are located within an n-dimensional space defined by the observations. Wickens (1995) argues that this version of the data space is actually more useful than the more typical representation (observation points within variable axes) because the analyst usually is more interested in the variables than in the individual observations. This alternative geometric representation of the data space is discussed in many texts on multivariate statistics, including Krzanowski (1990) and Fox (1997), as well as the presentation by Wickens (1995) mentioned above.

2. For an interesting, amusing, and thought-provoking discussion of these difficulties, see Abbott (1983).

3. All the graphs in this volume were created using S-Plus for Windows, Version 3.3 (both the high-level graphics routines and the Trellis Graphics System) and SYSTAT for Windows, Versions 5 and 6.

4. The data on state electorate ideologies and partisanship were provided by Gerald C. Wright. A detailed discussion and analysis of these variables can be found in Erikson, Wright, and McIver (1993).

5. Another related possibility would be to use different colors for encoding categories, if color is available in the display medium. For example, Cleveland (1994) suggests that dark blue (cyan), red (magenta), green, orange, and light blue are particularly effective (used in that order) to convey categorical distinctions in a graphical display.

6. The voting data were obtained from U.S. Bureau of the Census (1993).

7. These data were obtained from U.S. Department of Commerce (1993).

8. These data are from the Center for Political Studies' 1992 American National Election Study.

9. For example, *Chernoff faces* (Chernoff, 1973; Jacob, 1978) represent observations as cartoon faces, with the variable values encoded into the sizes and orientations of various facial features (such as the degree of smile/frown in the mouth, the position of the pupils within the eyes, the height of the eyebrows above the eyes, and so on). *Kleiner-Hartigan tree symbols* (Kleiner & Hartigan, 1981; Freni-Titulauer & Louv, 1984) show observations as icons with branches emanating from a central trunk. Each branch represents a variable; the placement of the branches within the tree (which remains the same across all the icons) depicts the relationships between the variables, whereas the length of a branch within a single tree shows the value of the corresponding variable for that observation.

10. The more "objective" seriation strategies, based on multivariate statistical methods, may seem to overcome this problem. It is important, however, to recognize that techniques such as principal components and multidimensional scaling are all based on particular models of variability (e.g., Jacoby, 1991). If the empirical data do not conform to these kinds of structures, then the resultant arrays of graphical components may not be particularly revealing of the true underlying structure within the data. Again, the best advice is simply to try a variety of different arrangements before selecting a "final" view of the data.

11. In more technical terms, the physical representation of the three-dimensional scatterplot is obtained by projecting a rotated, three-dimensional coordinate system onto the two-dimensional plane of the viewing surface. Scatterplot rotation is discussed in Becker, Cleveland, and Weil (1988); Buja, Asimov, Hurley, and McDonald (1988), and Cook and Weisberg (1994). The considerations involved in projecting multidimensional data onto two-dimensional viewing media are covered in Rogers and Adams (1990).

12. These data are adapted from information given in Lewis-Beck and Rice (1992).

13. These properties of a circle are not linearly related to each other, because the area is proportional to the square of the radius. Accordingly, areas increase at a faster rate than do the values of the diameters. Most of the software for creating bubble plots codes the third variable's value into the diameter of the circle, but this has an advantageous property: According to Stevens' (1975; also see Lodge, 1981) law of psychophysical perception, human observers systematically underestimate the relative areas of circles. If so, then the *perceived* areas of the bubbled plotting symbols should be closer to the actual values of the *diameters* than to the true areas. Therefore, the "consumers" of bubble plots should be encouraged to focus on the areas of the plotting symbols; their final judgments about the data values should be fairly accurate, despite the systematic perceptual biases that almost certainly will occur.

14. These data were obtained from the U.S. Bureau of the Census (1993).

15. One way to overcome this limitation would be to employ *scatterplot brushing* and related techniques in which the analyst interacts directly with the contents of the scatterplot matrix. Specifically, the graph is displayed on a computer screen, and a pointing device is used to highlight a subset of data points in one of the panels. The same observations are immediately highlighted in all other panels of the scatterplot matrix. This shows how observations vary across several variables simultaneously (Becker & Cleveland, 1987; Carr, Littlefield, Nicholson, & Littlefield, 1987; Cook & Weisberg, 1994).

16. These data were obtained from the Health Care Financing Administration, U.S. Department of Health and Human Services.

17. This kind of arrangement is called *main effects ordering* (Becker, Cleveland, & Shyu, 1995). Stated simply, the panels are laid out according to the central tendency of the values of the panel variable within each of the slices. This strategy provides a rational basis for arranging the panels of a conditioning plot whenever the conditioning variable is composed of nominal categories.

18. The casement plot requires a combination of textual and graphical information processing to deal with the panel labels and the contents of the dependence panels, respectively. The coplot relies primarily on graphical information processing, but the analyst must look back and forth between at least two distinct parts of the display—the dependence and given panels—to comprehend all the information. Finally, in the trellis display, the conditioning information is an integral part of each dependence panel; therefore, it is particularly easy to discern exactly which subset of the overall data are contained within each part of the display. For this reason, the trellis display strategy represents the most flexible type of conditioning plot.

19. This factorization also could be obtained simply by performing a principal components analysis on the data. The biplot would then be created by taking the variables' coefficients and the observations' scores on the first two principal components.

20. Although biplots based upon a singular value decomposition of a rectangular data matrix appear most frequently, there are many other types that could be created. In fact, any statistical procedure that generates two distinct sets of scores (i.e., for observations and variables, rows and columns, etc.) could be used to construct a biplot. For a detailed discussion of many different kinds of biplots, see Gower and Hand (1996).

21. Another possibility might be to construct a three-dimensional scatterplot that uses the scaled singular vectors to define a coordinate space containing variable vectors along with the observation points. All the perceptual problems discussed in Chapter 4, however, would also occur here. Furthermore, the pseudo-perspective view required for the visual display would inhibit accurate judgments about the sizes of angles between the vectors in the three-dimensional space. On the other hand, adding motion to a three-dimensional biplot (in the form of real-time, three-dimensional rotation) would decrease greatly any such problems.

22. Note that Table A.1 includes only methods that have been discussed in this monograph and its companion volume. Most of the software packages have other graphical features that are not covered here (e.g., contour plots, multivariate density estimation, and statistical maps). Many of the software packages also contain drawing tools that can be used to modify and customize graphical output.

23. Table A.1 is limited to software packages that are relatively general in their orientations; therefore, it omits several special-purpose programs that could be very useful for purposes of data visualization. These include the *R-Code* (Cook & Weisberg,

1994; Weisberg, 1996) for regression graphics and *XGobi* (Swayne, Cook, & Buja, n.d.) for high-dimensional rotation of multivariate data.

24. Kosslyn (1994) provides an excellent set of guidelines for selecting a graphics software package.

REFERENCES

ABBOTT, E. A. (1983) *Flatland: A Romance of Many Dimensions*. New York: Barnes and Noble.

ANDREWS, D. F. (1972) "Plots of high dimensional data." *Biometrics, 28,* 125-136.

ASIMOV, D. (1985) "The grand tour: A tool for viewing multidimensional data." *SIAM Journal of Scientific and Statistical Computing, 6,* 128-143.

BECKER, R. A., and CLEVELAND, W. S. (1987) "Brushing scatterplots." *Technometrics, 29,* 127-142.

BECKER, R. A., CLEVELAND, W. S., and SHYU, M.-J. (1995) *The Visual Design and Control of Trellis Display*. [Available on the World Wide Web at http:/netblib.bell-labs.com/cm/ms/departments/sia/project/trellis/].

BECKER, R. A. CLEVELAND, W. S., and WEIL, G. (1988) "The use of brushing and rotation for data analysis." In W. S. Cleveland and M. E. McGill (Eds.), *Dynamic Graphics for Statistics*. Belmont, CA: Wadsworth and Brooks/Cole.

BECKER, R. A., CLEVELAND, W. S., and WILKS, A. R. (1988) "Dynamic graphics for data analysis." In W.S. Cleveland and M. E. McGill (Eds.), *Dynamic Graphics for Statistics*. Belmont, CA: Wadsworth and Brooks/Cole.

BELLMAN, R. E. (1961) *Adaptive Control Processes*. Princeton, NJ: Princeton University Press.

BERTIN, J. (1983) *The Semiology of Graphs*. Madison, WI: University of Wisconsin Press.

BUJA, A., ASIMOV, D., HURLEY, C., and McDONALD, J. A. (1988) "Elements of a viewing pipeline for data analysis." In W.S. Cleveland and M. E. McGill (Eds.), *Dynamic Graphics for Statistics*. Belmont, CA: Wadsworth and Brooks/Cole.

CARR, D. B., LITTLEFIELD, R. J., NICHOLSON, W. L., and LITTLEFIELD, J. S. (1987) "Scatterplot matrix techniques for large N." *Journal of the American Statistical Association, 82,* 424-436.

CHAMBERS, J. M., CLEVELAND, W. S., KLEINER, B., and TUKEY, P. A. (1983) *Graphical Methods for Data Analysis*. Pacific Grove, CA: Wadsworth and Brooks/Cole.

CHERNOFF, H. (1973) "Using faces to represent points in k-dimensional space graphically." *Journal of the American Statistical Association, 68,* 361-368.

CLEVELAND, W. S. (1984) "Graphs in scientific publications." *The American Statistician, 38,* 270-280.

CLEVELAND, W. S. (1993a) "A model for studying display methods of statistical graphics." *Journal of Computational and Graphical Statistics, 2,* 323-343.

CLEVELAND, W. S. (1993b) *Visualizing Data*. Summit, NJ: Hobart Press.

CLEVELAND, W. S. (1994) *The Elements of Graphing Data* (Rev. ed.). Summit, NJ: Hobart Press.

CLEVELAND, W. S., DEVLIN, S. J., and GROSSE, E. (1988) "Regression by local fitting: Methods, properties, and computational algorithms." *Journal of Econometrics, 37*, 87-114.

CLEVELAND, W. S., McGILL, M. E., & McGILL, R. (1988) "The shape parameter of a two-variable graph." *Journal of the American Statistical Association, 83*, 289-300.

COOK, R. D., and WEISBERG, S. (1994) *Introduction to Regression Graphics.* New York: John Wiley and Sons.

DUNTEMAN, G. H. (1989) *Principal Components Analysis.* Newbury Park, CA: Sage.

ECKART, C., and YOUNG, G. (1936) "The approximation of one matrix by another of lower rank." *Psychometrika, 1*, 211-218.

ERIKSON, R. S., WRIGHT, G. C., and McIVER, J. P. (1993) *Statehouse Democracy: Public Opinion and Public Policy in the American States.* Cambridge, UK: Cambridge University Press.

FOX, J. (1997) *Applied Regression Analysis, Linear Models, and Related Methods.* Thousand Oaks, CA: Sage.

FOX, J., and FRIENDLY, M. (1996) "Data analysis using APL2 and APL2STAT." In R. Stine and J. Fox (Eds.), *Statistical Computing Environments for Social Research.* Thousand Oaks, CA: Sage.

FRENI-TITULAUER, L. W. J., and LOUV, W. C. (1984) "Comparisons of some graphical methods for exploratory multivariate data analysis." *The American Statistician, 38*, 184-188.

FRIEDMAN, H. P., FARRELL, E. S., GOLDWYN, R. M., MILLER, M., and SIGEL, J. (1972) "A graphic way of describing changing multivariate patterns." *Proceedings of the Sixth Interface Symposium on Computer Science and Statistics.* Berkeley: University of California Press.

FRIEDMAN, J. H. (1987) "Exploratory projection pursuit." *Journal of the American Statistical Association, 82*, 249-266.

FRIENDLY, M. (1991) *SAS System for Statistical Graphics.* Cary, NC: SAS Institute.

FRIENDLY, M. (1994) "Mosaic displays for n-way contingency tables." *Journal of the American Statistical Association, 89*, 190-200.

GABRIEL, K. R. (1971) "The biplot graphical display of matrices with application to principal component analysis." *Biometrika, 58*, 453-467.

GABRIEL, K. R. (1981) "Biplot display of multivariate matrices for inspection of data and diagnosis." In V. Barnett (Ed.), *Interpreting Multivariate Data.* Chichester, UK: John Wiley and Sons.

GNANADESIKAN, R. (1997) *Methods for Statistical Analysis of Multivariate Observations.* New York: John Wiley and Sons.

GOWER, J. C., and DIGBY, P. G. N. (1981) "Expressing complex relationships in two dimensions." In V. Barnett (Ed.), *Interpreting Multivariate Data.* Chichester, UK: John Wiley and Sons.

GOWER, J. C., and HAND, D. J. (1996) *Biplots.* London: Chapman and Hall.

GREEN, P. E., and CARROLL, J. D. (1976) *Mathematical Tools for Applied Multivariate Analysis.* New York: Academic Press.

GREENACRE, M. J. (1984) *Theory and Applications of Correspondence Analysis.* London: Academic Press.

HARTIGAN, J. A., and KLEINER, B. (1981) "Mosaics for contingency tables." *Computer Science and Statistics: Proceedings of the 13th Symposium on the Interface.* New York: Springer-Verlag.

HUBER, P. J. (1985) "Projection pursuit." *The Annals of Statistics, 13,* 435-475.

HUBER, P. J. (1987) "Experiences with three-dimensional scatterplots." *Journal of the American Statistical Association, 82,* 448-452.

HUFF, D. (1954) *How to lie with statistics.* New York: W. W. Norton.

HURLEY, C., and BUJA, A. (1990) "Analyzing high-dimensional data with motion graphics." *SIAM Journal of Scientific and Statistical Computing, 11,* 1193-1211.

INSELBERG, A. (1985) "The plane with parallel coordinates." *The Visual Computer, 1,* 69-91.

JACOB, R. J. K. (1978) "Facial representation of multivariate data." In P. C. C. Wang (Ed.), *Graphical Representation of Multivariate Data.* New York: Academic Press.

JACOBY, W. G. (1991) *Data Theory and Dimensional Analysis.* Newbury Park, CA: Sage.

JACOBY, W. G. (1997) *Statistical Graphics for Visualizing Univariate and Bivariate Data.* Thousand Oaks, CA: Sage.

KLEINER, B., and HARTIGAN, J. A. (1981) "Representing points in many dimensions by trees and castles." *Journal of the American Statistical Association, 76,* 260-276.

KOSSLYN, S. M. (1994) *Elements of Graph Design.* New York: W. H. Freeman.

KRZANOWSKI, W. J. (1990) *Principles of Multivariate Analysis: A User's Perspective.* Oxford, UK: Oxford University Press.

LEWIS-BECK, M. S., and RICE, T. W. (1992) *Forecasting Elections.* Washington, DC: Congressional Quarterly.

LODGE, M. (1981) *Magnitude Scaling.* Beverly Hills, CA: Sage.

NICHOLSON, W. L., and LITTLEFIELD, R. J. (1983) "Interactive color graphics for multivariate data." In K. W. Heiner, R. S. Sacher, and J. W. Wilkinson (Eds.), *Computer Science and Statistics: Proceedings of the 14th Symposium on the Interface.* New York: Springer-Verlag.

ROCK, I. (1984) *Perception.* New York: Scientific American Books.

ROGERS, D. F., and ADAMS, J. A. (1990) *Mathematical Elements for Computer Graphics* (2nd ed.). New York: McGraw-Hill.

SCHMID, C. F. (1983) *Statistical Graphics: Design Principles and Practices.* New York: John Wiley and Sons.

SCHMID, C. F., and SCHMID, S. E. (1979) *Handbook of Graphic Presentation.* New York: John Wiley and Sons.

SIMONOFF, J. S. (1996) *Smoothing Methods in Statistics.* New York: Springer-Verlag.

SNEATH, P. H., and SOKAL, R. R. (1973) *Numerical Taxonomy.* San Francisco: W. H. Freeman.

STEVENS, S. S. (1975) *Psychophysics.* New York: John Wiley and Sons.

STINE, R., and FOX, J. (Eds.). (1996) *Statistical Computing Environments for Social Research.* Thousand Oaks, CA: Sage.

STUETZLE, W. (1987) "Plot windows." *Journal of the American Statistical Association, 82,* 466-475.

SWAYNE, D., COOK, D., and BUJA, A. (n.d.) *XGobi.* [Computer program available on the World Wide Web at www.stat.cmu.edu/general/XGobi].

TIERNEY, L. (1990) *Lisp-Stat: An Object-Oriented Environment for Statistical Computing and Dynamic Graphics.* New York: John Wiley and Sons.

TUFTE, E. R. (1983) *The Visual Display of Quantitative Information.* Cheshire, CT: Graphics Press.

TUFTE, E. R. (1990) *Envisioning Information.* Cheshire, CT: Graphics Press.

TUFTE, E. R. (1997) *Visual Explanations.* Cheshire, CT: Graphics Press.

102

TUKEY, P. A., and TUKEY, J. W. (1981) "Graphical display of data sets in 3 or more dimensions." In V. Barnett (Ed.), *Interpreting Multivariate Data.* Chichester, UK: John Wiley and Sons.

U.S. BUREAU OF THE CENSUS. (1993) *Statistical Abstract of the United States: 1993* (113th ed.). Washington, DC: Government Printing Office.

U.S. DEPARTMENT OF COMMERCE. (1993) *State Government Finances: 1992.* Washington, DC: U.S. Bureau of the Census.

WAINER, H. (1997) *Visual Revelations.* New York: Copernicus.

WAINER, H., and THISSEN, D. (1981) "Graphical data analysis." *Annual Review of Psychology, 32,* 191-241.

WEGMAN, E. J. (1990) "Hyperdimensional data analysis using parallel coordinates." *Journal of the American Statistical Association, 85,* 664-675.

WEISBERG, H. F. (1974) "Dimensionland: An excursion into spaces." *American Journal of Political Science, 18,* 743-776.

WEISBERG, H. F. (1996) "The R-code: A graphical paradigm for regression analysis." In R. Stine and J. Fox (Eds.), *Statistical Computing Environments for Social Research.* Thousand Oaks, CA: Sage.

WELLER, S., and ROMNEY, A. K. (1990) *Metric Scaling: Correspondence Analysis.* Newbury Park, CA: Sage.

WICKENS, T. D. (1995) *The Geometry of Multivariate Statistics.* Hillsdale, NJ: Lawrence Erlbaum.

WILKINSON, L., HILL, M., MICELLI, S., BIRKENBEUEL, G., and VANG, E. (1992) *Systat for Windows: Graphics, Version 5 Edition.* Evanston, IL: SYSTAT, Inc.

YOUNG, F. W. (1987) "Theory." In F. W. Young and R. M. Hamer (Eds.), *Multidimensional Scaling.* Hillsdale, NJ: Lawrence Erlbaum.

YOUNG, F. W. (1997) *ViSta: The Visual Statistics System.* Chapel Hill, NC: L. L. Thurstone Psychometrics Laboratory.

YOUNG, F. W., and RHEINGANS, P. (1991) "Visualizing structure in high-dimensional multivariate data." *IBM Journal of Research and Development, 35,* 97-107.

YOUNG, F. W., FALDOWSKI, R. A., and HARRIS, D. F. (1990) "The SpreadPlot: A graphical spreadsheet with algebraically linked dynamic plots." *Proceedings: The American Statistical Association Section on Statistical Graphics,* 42-47.

YOUNG, F. W., FALDOWSKI, R. A., and McFARLANE, M. M. (1993) "Multivariate statistical visualization." In C. R. Rao (Ed.), *Handbook of Statistics, Volume 9.* New York: Elsevier.

YOUNG, F. W., KENT, D. P., and KUHFELD, W. F. (1988) "Dynamic graphics for exploring multivariate data." In W. S. Cleveland and M. E. McGill (Eds.), *Dynamic Graphics for Statistics.* Belmont, CA: Wadsworth and Brooks/Cole.

ABOUT THE AUTHOR

WILLIAM G. JACOBY is Associate Professor in the Department of Government and International Studies at the University of South Carolina. He received his BA from the University of Delaware, and his MA and PhD in Political Science from the University of North Carolina at Chapel Hill. Along with statistical graphics, his major areas of interest include measurement and scaling methods, public opinion, and political behavior. Dr. Jacoby is the author of *Data Theory and Dimensional Analysis* and has published articles in such journals as the *American Journal of Political Science*, the *Journal of Politics*, and *Political Analysis*.